PUFFIN BOOKS

Edit

T

In *The Marsh* magnificent stor *The Namesake.* Alfred and the lea council as to how they shoulc with the Danish leader Guthorm and his vikings, whom they had at last surrounded in their camp.

'Let the heathen be slain, every one of them,' said Odda.

'Rather, let them starve,' said Alfgar.

But the king said, 'If we slay these four hundred, what good will it do us? There are ten times as many more in the north eager and ready to take their places.

'Let them go back to their fellows in the north. Let them say that we in Wessex can afford to be generous because we are a strong nation and cannot be conquered.'

So Guthorm and his Danes went free, only to return and strike again in mid-winter, with a treacherous plot to kill the king. And for a while Guthorm believed his great adversary had really been slain at his nephew's wedding feast, until rumours began to reach him of a Marsh king, who was slowly gathering his forces in an impregnable position, ready for a final blow against the Danes. And this time Alfred thought he would succeed.

For older Puffin readers.

The Marsh King

*

Written and illustrated by

C. WALTER HODGES

PENGUIN BOOKS

Penguin Books Ltd, Harmondsworth, Middlesex, England
Penguin Books Australia Ltd, Ringwood, Victoria, Australia

—

First published by G. Bell 1967
Published in Puffin Books 1970

—

—

Made and printed in Great Britain by
Hazell Watson & Viney Ltd, Aylesbury, Bucks
Set in Monotype Plantin

FOR LETTY

Contents

CONTENTS

CHAPTER ONE

The Witnesses

ATHELSTAN REDBEARD the Dane, King of East Anglia, died suddenly, sitting upright upon his horse, when I was two years old. He was my godfather, so my mother told me; but I have heard that he considered it his right to be godfather to all the children born at his court, so this was a distinction I shared with many. Once every year, on the anniversary of his own baptism, he held a great christening feast in his hall. There my grandfather, Olaf the Skald, would sing the long story of the King's deeds and battles, as he himself had known them, having stood beside him both as pagan and Christian through most of them. I remember my grandfather well, his wiry hands upon the harp, his thin strong voice singing through the nose. My father, Skafti Olafsson, when little more than a boy had been with my grandfather in the harrying of Wessex, and though he was not himself a skald he knew all the old man's verses, and could add others of his own. From these two in my childhood I learned many of the things I shall here relate.

My mother's father, a thane of the West Saxons, Unferth by name, brought shame upon our family through his treachery; but a certain deed of my mother's restored honour to us. Of this you shall learn. She was a little girl at the time of this story. Her name was Hildis. The things I shall tell are as she told them to me.

Also, there was living here in East Anglia until a few years ago a very old man who in his younger days had known King Alfred of Wessex, and had served him at court and in the field of battle. This man was not a warrior, but a scribe. His name also was Alfred, as was the King's and he was known as Dane-Leg; for he had only one leg; the other had been cut off by the heathen, it was said, when he was a child. For this reason in later life he had made himself a leg from the shaft of a heathen spear, and so had earned the name of Dane-Leg.

This old man I met five summers ago. I wished to learn from him about King Alfred, to add to what I already knew, having it in mind to write this story. So I travelled to the monastery at St Edmund's Minster in East Anglia, where the old man then lived. I found him in a little room, asleep by the window. A warm breeze from the orchard outside moved his long white hairs against his cheek, and rustled the parchment upon the table at his side. I saw an old crutch standing in the corner, and I saw his one foot upon the footstool. When he woke I told him who I was, and why I had come. He said:

'I am nearly blind now, and I see you only as a shape against the wall. But let that not matter. I can still remember King Alfred's face well enough, feature by feature. I see him more clearly in my mind's eye than I see you yourself standing in the flesh before me. It is a happy day for me that sends you here. I must tell you that some years ago I myself began to write a book about King Alfred. But then my sight began to darken, and I could find no one at hand to continue where I left off. At my age one grows quickly tired, and perhaps I did not seek far or hard enough for helpers. God has now sent you to stir my memory again.'

He gave me to take away and read what he had already written, and thereafter we talked together many times. Before I left him for the last time he asked me to take down from the wall a leather wallet that was hanging there, and from this he drew out several old pens of goose-quill, mostly very shortened from cutting, and each having a character of its own, as pens have. He felt each with his fingers till he found the one he sought. Then he asked for my writing hand, and between the fingers of it he placed this pen saying: 'This was the pen with which I wrote the last words of my book. Let it serve to write the first words of your own.' This I have done.

CHAPTER TWO

Ethelbalt's Conspiracy

IT was in the time of King Ethelwulf, King Alfred's father, that the pagans first began to settle in England. Before this, frequent as they were, their raids had been short. They would come with some twenty or thirty ships, to burn and kill, take their plunder, and make off. But in King Ethelwulf's time their ships were numbered in hundreds, and wherever they landed they meant to stay. In Wessex King Ethelwulf and his thanes met them shield to shield. Many battles were fought, and many fields were left thick with pagan dead. They had short shrift in Wessex; but elsewhere, in Mercia, East Anglia and Northumbria, along all the coast, and in ancient Ireland, once so rich with treasure, the armed heathen gathered in their thousands, like starlings on the rooftops in autumn watching the red sun go down.

'Darkness is creeping over all the world we have known,' King Ethelwulf said, 'and it seems that not all our valour in battle is enough to prevent it. Here am I in my fiftieth year, and for twenty-five of those years I have had these heathen on my threshold. Had I done in the beginning what I am now going to do, much evil might have been averted.'

So he prepared to make a pilgrimage to Rome, to pray there at the shrines of the apostles, and to do penance for his sins and for the sins of his people which he knew had been the true cause of this heathen plague, surely sent as a punishment from God. In making this pilgrimage he was carrying out the advice of his priests and bishops, which he followed to the letter; and for good measure before he went he bequeathed a tenth part of all his lands and goods into the hands of the Church.

With him on his journey he took his youngest son Alfred, his favourite, who was then only six years old. To his eldest son Ethelbalt he left the care of his kingdom while he was away. He did not expect to return for a year or more. It is a long and difficult journey.

This Ethelbalt was a thin and handsome man, proud of his hawks and his horses and his rich clothing. Nothing pleased him more than to have the kingdom in his charge at last. He had chafed for a long time under his father's rule, as the old man grew older and more pious. 'Even the stables begin to smell of incense,' Ethelbalt had said, scornfully. His father knew him to be ambitious and impatient, but he was the eldest son and he trusted him. He also trusted in the wisdom and experience of two great men of Wessex, Ealstan, bishop of Sherborne, and Eanwulf, ealdorman of Somerset, to guide his son in the affairs of the kingdom. He could hardly have done worse.

I speak no ill of Bishop Ealstan. He was very old and may have been deceived, though some say he had always been cunning as a fox. But that Eanwulf of Somerset was a traitor to a good king, and Ethelbalt an unworthy son to a good father, these things cannot be denied. However, King Ethelwulf acted unwisely, and gave them some cause for their action, as will be seen shortly.

The King remained many months in Rome. He did penance, he gave great gifts of gold to the Church and to the clergy of St Peter, he scattered silver among the people of the city, he held conference with the Holy Father and was blessed by him, together with Alfred the young prince. Then at last he began the long journey home, first by ship to Massilia and so northward through France until he came to where the Emperor Charles held court in his new palace at Verberium, near Reims. Here for his grief he found messengers from Wessex awaiting him, with the news that his wife Osburga was dead and buried during his long absence. He mourned for her with Alfred his son in the Emperor's chapel at Verberium. And thereafter he remained with the Emperor till spring lengthened into summer.

In Wessex the Atheling Ethelbalt did not welcome the news that his father was at last on his way home. He said: 'He has stayed long, lingering now in one place now in another, giving little care to his kingdom. Let him stay longer. We who have managed so much for him can manage more.' Eanwulf the ealdorman, who had a great following among the thanes of Wessex, gathered many friends into this opinion, to their shame. But many at first were doubtful. Bishop Ealstan would not commit himself. 'The King has behaved well,' said he. 'In Rome he has atoned for his people's sins, and in Paris we now learn he is forging strong chains of friendship with the Emperor. Hardly good reasons, either of them, to keep him from his throne and country.'

But when further news came, telling what bond it was that the King had made with the Emperor, the bishop and others changed their tune. Eanwulf had sent a young man of his following to spy upon the King in France and bring him early news. This man was called Unferth. He was a person of small inheritance, eager to earn his way to thanehood by any means, and he saw now that by serving the ambitions of Eanwulf, whatever they might be, he might quickly advance his own. Unferth came hotfoot from France, and found his master at Winchester with the Atheling. He told them that the old king had married again. His bride was Judith, the Emperor's daughter, a child of only thirteen.

Atheling Ethelbalt smote the table with his fist, and cried: 'Tell that, then, to my thanes in the Council! Now let them learn who is fit to rule in Wessex and who is not!'

Bishop Ealstan was told. He said: 'The King has neither sense nor decency. Besides, who knows what this will mean in the dividing of his estates, if he has more children. He is not wise.'

'He is an old fool,' the Atheling said, 'and he shames us. He shall not set foot here again.'

But this, in spite of everything Ealdorman Eanwulf and the others could do, was still beyond their power to prevent. The King had other sons who did not see eye to eye with Ethelbalt, and there were other thanes less treacherous than Eanwulf. However, when the King landed at Dover at midsummer, leading the little girl, his queen, by the hand, he found his country divided against itself. Meanwhile, on the north wind people could smell the foul stench of the heathen clustered in their thousands just beyond the borders of Wessex, waiting for the rival parties to finish each other off in civil war, so that they could then come in and gather up the spoils.

CHAPTER THREE

Queen Judith

QUEEN JUDITH had wept bitterly to leave her father's court and all her childhood friends, and go across the dark sea into the land of the West Saxons. During all the long journey she had determined she would say not a single word to her old husband; she would refuse even to look at him. But as it happened he did not come near her. He rode a mile ahead with his thane-guard. She travelled in a great painted waggon, drawn by six oxen, with embroidered curtains which she kept drawn and fastened. With her she had her waiting-maid Waltruda, a girl only a little older than herself; and sometimes for other company they had the little prince Alfred to ride along with them. He was not unfriendly to his new stepmother, who truth to tell was more of an age to be his playmate.

They were all day sailing to Dover. The wind was contrary, the sea rough, and Queen Judith felt very ill. When the ship was pulled ashore and a platform had been set for her to walk down, old King Ethelwulf came for her at last and took her by the hand, and led her out among the wide-faced yellow-headed Saxons, who treated her either too coldly or too kindly, and spoke of her not as a Queen, daughter of an imperial house, but as 'the Frankish girl'.

On the day after landing they rode to Canterbury in warm weather. Queen Judith was lodged in a house that looked across the fields to Saint Augustine's Abbey. She saw the nobles of Wessex tethering their horses there, coming to meet the old king in council in the Abbey courtyard. It was a momentous day for Wessex. The King showed great wisdom. He said he would not foster discord in his own land against his own son.

He offered to share the kingdom with Ethelbalt, himself to rule over the eastern half of it, resigning all the western part to his son. He did this in wisdom and sincerity, to avoid bloodshed; and it was wisely accepted. Ethelbalt came to Canterbury with Eanwulf, and Ealstan the bishop, and all their thanes, and he knelt in the Abbey beside his father and brothers, and Ceolnoth the Archbishop returned thanks to God for their reconciliation. Then the King held a feast at Canterbury. He had a high seat prepared on a dais in the hall, for himself and the lady Judith, who sat there beside him as Queen. This was not the Saxon custom for a King's wife to do, and the thanes did not like it; but Ethelwulf did it to please his young bride. At this feast for the first time she came face to face with her stepson Ethelbalt. She thought him very handsome, and carried the mead-cup to him, next after her husband, in the manner of Saxon women to the honoured guest. Ethelbalt smiled at her, showing his white teeth, but she discreetly did not raise her eyes.

So the peace was made and kept. Thereafter Queen Judith lived mostly at the King's vill at Guildford, with Waltruda her companion. The time passed slowly for them among the women of the household. King Ethelwulf rarely came to the vill. Affairs of state and religion were all that concerned him now. His marriage had been a matter of policy, not of love, though he liked the little girl well enough, as a father might. She did not know that he was sick.

Meanwhile Ethelbalt in his western kingship hunted and flew his hawks, and spread the gay cloak of his youth in the summer pastures. Eanwulf of Somerset and Bishop Ealstan were at his right and his left hand in the Council, whenever he chose to attend it. Eanwulf made enemies there, but his power was great and he could afford to disregard them.

At a time when the young Queen, his stepmother, was staying at Farnham, not far from the boundary of the divided kingdom, King Ethelbalt went hunting in the hills of Hampshire nearby, and killed many deer, which he took to her as a gift, going with them himself into his father's domain. He stayed there a day and a night, and Ethelwulf was not present. When he returned to his own place Ealdorman Eanwulf heard of it.

'Let me advise you, my lord,' said he. 'Such conduct will give rise to scandal, and may break the peace. We are very well off as we are. You should be more careful.'

'You will soon become old, like my father,' said Ethelbalt. 'Old people have no sap, their advice is dry, and I can do without it.'

Eanwulf became red in the face with anger. 'King,' he said, 'if you will not be advised, be warned. The thanes of Wessex are still of two minds between yourself and your father. Do not provoke trouble.'

Ethelbalt laughed and went out. Less than a month after this they learned that the King his father was dead, and his body was being brought to Winchester for burial. The Queen stood at the graveside, near to Ethelbalt and his three brothers. Of these the eldest, Ethelbert, was then seventeen years of age, and the youngest, Alfred, only nine. Ethelbalt thought now he would have all Wessex for his own, but the thanes of Kent and Sussex would not hear of it. They at once named his brother Ethelbert king over the eastern shires, in his father's place.

As Queen Judith and her train were returning towards Farnham from Winchester, after the funeral, King Ethelbalt overtook them on the road. She opened the curtains of her waggon.

'Lady,' he said, 'you are still in my own territory here, and you have no need to leave unless you wish. Will you not accept hospitality from me?'

Judith said demurely: 'Whether he be dead or alive I belong to my husband and his people. I must go where I belong.'

'I will see about that,' said Ethalbalt. Six months later, or less as some have said, he took her for his own wife.

I do not need to describe the disgust which was felt in every part of Wessex at such an impious deed. The marriage was solemnized by King Ethelbalt's own mass-priest, with none but the thanes of his household to witness it, for no bishop in the land would do it, not even old Ealstan of Sherborne, who had borne with the evil ways of King Ethelbalt for long enough. He withdrew in horror from the King's court, and never went there thereafter. In France, Archbishop Hincmar of Reims who had solemnised Judith's first marriage two years before, now reproved her father the Emperor for this one, almost as if he had himself committed the sin. To marry her own stepson! Ealdorman Eanwulf, who had linked his fortunes so firmly with Ethelbalt's that he could not now withdraw, had cause to feel uneasy. But this presently passed. He said to his man Unferth:

'They are both young and have long to live. People will soon forget about this so-called sin. It was a greater sin to marry her to that old man in the first place.'

'People are saying it will bring a curse upon the land,' said Unferth.

'There is always some curse or other upon the land,' said Eanwulf, 'and people will always find some reason for it, whether there is a reason or not. People are fools. This does not worry me.'

He was worried, however, for another reason. He had many enemies and very few friends, and King Ethelbalt's friendship now looked as if it would be unsteady. If Eanwulf for any reason should lose the King's favour he might soon lose much else besides. His wife and property would not be safe. He said to Unferth:

'I am your lord, and know what things you expect of me. You hope to buy land with gifts, so as to increase your blood-price, so that your sons, when you have them, may become thanes. I can help you to all this. But what will you do for me?'

'You are my lord,' said Unferth, 'and therefore I stand beside you to do whatever service a free man may do, even to death.'

Said Eanwulf: 'Not death but marriage is what I have in mind. If I am now to keep close to the King I shall need friends who are close to the Queen. What do you think of Waltruda, the Queen's waiting-woman?'

Unferth made no reply, but waited, and Eanwulf continued:

'She and Queen Judith are dear to each other. You are young and not ill-made. You should have a wife, and Waltruda has no husband. Why not you?'

So Eanwulf gave Unferth embroidered clothes and gold armlets and a fine harness for his horse, and Unferth rode with him to King Ethelbalt's palace at Sherborne. A gay company was gathered there. Ethelbalt and his young companions spent their days in sport and hunting in Selwood Forest. There he was having built as a wedding gift for his Queen a royal house, in a valley on the edge of the forest, by a stream called Alham. It was an estate which had belonged to the great King Egbert, Ethelbalt's grandfather; and an old hall which King Egbert had built as a hunting lodge stood darkly in the woods nearby.

During the whole of one year while the young King and his Queen sported and spent the wealth of their estates in West Wessex, the power and riches of Ealdorman Eanwulf increased. In the spring Unferth was married to Waltruda, and the King attended the ceremony. Eanwulf there gave to the King a black stallion named Mokkurkalfi, which he knew the King coveted.

At the New Year Queen Judith gave birth to a son, whom she named Edgar. At the christening feast King Ethelbalt became drunk. He ordered Mokkurkalfi to be saddled, and with whipping and shouting he rode it round and around outside the feast-hall, making it leap and rear up. Then he rode it through the doors into the hall between the long tables. The thanes beat upon the tables with their fists, and blew horns. Then, becoming frightened among the crowds, and with all the noise and the smoke and the fire upon the hearth, and being already angry from the whip, the great horse suddenly reared up and screamed and threw King Ethelbalt full against one of the pillars of the hall. When they went to pick him up they found the king was dead, his neck broken in two.

CHAPTER FOUR

Waltruda

WHEN Charles, Emperor of the Franks, heard that his daughter was widowed once more, young as she was, he sent immediately for her to return to France. This she was only too glad to do, for she knew she had no friends among the Saxons. The people of Wessex now wanted to forget Ethelbalt and his shameful conspiracy, which had cut the kingdom in two, and they had no use for his shameful Frankish queen. No time was lost in uniting the kingdom again under the rule of her husband's brother Ethelbert. Meanwhile, Ealdorman Eanwulf's fears had proved only too well-founded. His enemies lay in wait for him as he came ashore from a boat near Glastonbury, with only three companions, with whom he had been trapping wildfowl on the Marsh; and there they killed him, not six months after Ethelbalt's death. Unferth brought the news to the Queen and Waltruda.

Waltruda asked: 'And where were you, then, when this happened? Where were all his faithful companions, who should have guarded him with their lives?'

'Wife, I would have died with him, as did the three who were with him, had I been there,' said Unferth. 'But now I have a duty to preserve my own life till I can avenge his blood. Hold your peace.'

Judith had feared she would be left in Wessex a pauper without either friends or property, but King Ethelbert allowed her to keep the estate at Alham which his brother had given her. Here she was living when the messengers came from the Emperor to conduct her back to France.

'But, Lady,' said they, 'your father commands that you must

not bring your child with you. At some later time he may be sent for. We know the natural sorrow this must bring to a mother's heart, but the Emperor has his reasons.'

So Queen Judith returned to France leaving the baby Edgar to be nursed at Alham. It happened that Waltruda at about that time had given birth to a child that was still-born, so she took Judith's baby instead, and nursed it, and remained at Alham with her husband Unferth. She expected sorrowfully as the months went by that at any time messengers would come from France to take her nurseling from her; but none came.

Queen Judith had been sent by her father to live at Senlis, where she was well guarded. The Emperor did not want to hear any more about her affairs in Wessex, nor of her Saxon child; neither did he intend to give her any freedom to bring further shame upon his house. Nonetheless, before two years had passed she had run off with the young Count of Flanders, Baldwin, called Iron-Arm, and after much trouble, and with the Pope himself as mediator, the Emperor had had to accept it and become reconciled to his daughter's third marriage. Soon Judith in Flanders had other children to care for, and in the meanwhile Waltruda had grown to love her nurseling. So the child Edgar grew up at Alham Vill, carrying the royal blood of the Franks and the West Saxons in his veins. In his mother's name the vill belonged to him; but while he was young the Lady Waltruda governed both him and it.

Unferth came and went. It was not to his liking that his wife should rule the vill over his head, but it had come about in that way since at first he had not dared to stay there, for his life. There was now a new ealdorman in Somerset, in Eanwulf's place. This was Ethelnoth, who later stood through great troubles at King Alfred's right hand, as shall be told. But he was Unferth's enemy, since Unferth had been Eanwulf's man. There was a blood-feud between Ethelnoth's kin and Eanwulf's and therefore between all their people. Unferth had thought it prudent to leave Wessex for a time. He travelled north into

Mercia and Northumbria, and at another time, later, he went to Flanders to the court of Count Baldwin, where he saw the Countess Judith with her children. She sighed when he mentioned Edgar, her firstborn, and gave presents for Unferth to take to him; but no more than that. Unferth saw that she was well satisfied as Countess of Flanders, and that she did not wish to alter things. When he returned to Alham he said to Waltruda:

'You are mistress here for as long as you please, it seems to me. But as for me, I am a lordless man, neither churl nor thane, living here in your shadow.'

Said Waltruda: 'When my foster-son is old enough, will he not be your rightful lord, and will it not be an honour for you to serve him? He is the only son of the eldest son of the royal house of Wessex. One day the crown may be his. Have you thought of that?'

'I have thought of it,' said Unferth, 'but that day is a long way off. In any case, while his uncles live, there is little chance it will come at all.'

'But what if they do *not* live?' asked Waltruda. 'There is a sickness in them all. Is not Ethelbert dead already? He seemed in good health when he took his brother's place on the throne; then suddenly he sickened and died. And Alfred, the youngest brother, is likely to do the same. They say he already has a dizzy, sweating sickness which comes over him at unexpected times, so that he often cannot stand on his feet for as much as two days together. He may not live long; or, if he does, he is more likely to become a monk than a king. I have known him since he was a boy, and I know his nature. That leaves only Ethelred, who now wears the crown. If he should die, would not the crown come to Edgar?'

'If, if,' said Unferth. 'It is a useless word.'

'Misfortunes happen, even to kings,' said Waltruda. 'Ethelbalt broke his neck. Even if King Ethelred does not die of a sickness, he may soon die in battle, if what you say is true.'

'I have not said such a thing.'

'You have said you think it will not be long before the Northmen break Wessex, as they have already broken Mercia and Northumbria. You say you have seen their ships hunting like packs of wolves around the coasts of Wessex. You say you have seen their armies on land, and that nothing can stand against them. Can King Ethelred stand against them?'

'And supposing he cannot, what then?' asked Unferth. 'Will Edgar fare better with the heathen than Ethelred can? You make too much of this.'

'Edgar is my foster-son, and he is made of the blood of Kings,' said Waltruda. 'I myself make nothing of it but what there is.'

It was true that Unferth had seen the Northmen on sea and land. He knew them well. He had had dealings with them in some sort of trade while he was in Mercia.

'They are not bad fellows,' he was sometimes heard to say. 'They are brutish and greedy and cruel, but otherwise they are not bad fellows.'

Shortly after the conversation with Waltruda which has just been related, Unferth went away again into Mercia, saying it was uncertain when he would return. It was four years before he was again at Alham.

Meanwhile Waltruda continued as before to manage the estate in the name of her foster-son Edgar, who was now seven years old. But by this time she also had children of her own. She had two sons, Elric and Elred. And soon after Unferth's departure she gave birth to her last child, a daughter whom she named Hildis. This was Hildis who married Skafti Olaffson the Dane and became my mother.

CHAPTER FIVE

The Dragon Hall

THE vill at Alham stood at a place on the forest's edge where a little brook from a steep valley of the wood came out from the trees and joined the Alham stream. The houses of the vill were built on rising ground in the crook where the two streams joined. The hall, with its bowers, and other buildings, all enclosed by a high wooden fence, stood at the centre. This hall was built of stone, which King Ethelbalt had had quarried twenty miles away at Ham, and brought all that distance at great cost to please his Frankish queen; for she had told him of the palaces of carved stone in her homeland, and therefore he would not use timber for the hall, though all the trees of Selwood were at hand. All around, however, the other buildings were of wood. There were dwelling houses, stables, a dairy, granaries and barns, and, by the stream, a smithy and a mill. Fields, meadows and orchards lay on both sides of the river downstream for more than a mile. On the upper slopes, westward, were rough pasture lands. Eastward lay the forest. The hearth-smoke from the many roofs of the vill rose upward like pale pathways against the dark trees.

Across the brook and uphill a track led for half a mile into the forest. Here, at the far side of an open space stood the old dwelling-hall which King Egbert had built there, sixty years before. It was surrounded by a high hedge of quick-thorn, dense and black, forming a courtyard in which were a number of out-buildings. Over the hedge from the outside all that could be seen was the great gabled roof of the hall, the gable-ends crossed like horns above the roof-ridge. The timbers of the gables had been carved into the shapes of enormous dragons twisted together, and for this reason the place was called the Dragon Hall. But it had stood for a long time deserted. Its timbers were dark and cracked, the thatch was rotten and partly fallen into holes. The place had been used for storage and shelter from time to time, but after a herdsman's fire had accidentally burned down one of the huts, the reeve at the vill ordered the courtyard to be closed and sealed, so that no one could get in.

Here on a summer evening Waltruda's children came wandering up from the stream. Elric the eldest was nine years old, Elred seven. An older boy from the vill, the falconer's son Duri, was with them, carrying Hildis on his shoulders. She was then only four.

This was the summer of the year when the pagan army first broke into Wessex, when they camped at Reading and burnt Wilton and fought five great battles against the West Saxons, but could not beat them. This was the year when King Ethelred died of his wounds and King Alfred took his place. This was the summer when the pagans had at last agreed to a truce and for the time being had marched away with their spoils, while the Saxons buried their dead and carried the wounded home to their farms. But not any of the battle or the marching had come near this quiet part of Selwood. The little summertime gnats danced in the sunlight above the wandering children, who stood and gazed at the dragon gables showing over the thorn hedge at the far side of the clearing.

Presently the children went nearer. They followed the hedge around for part of the way till they came to the gate. There were some chinks between the timbers through which they could see in. Among the deserted buildings everything was still, except for the dancing gnats.

'There's a dead pig in there,' said Duri. They pushed to get at the chink through which it could be seen. Elric said:

'There's another pig on the far side. It's alive. It's only a pigling. Now it's gone behind the house.' They now saw that

the first one was not dead, but only asleep. Duri said he would climb the gate and get into the courtyard, but in the end he could find no way to do it. So they wandered a little way into the wood, and as they did so they saw a young pig run out from a bush. Leaving Hildis alone the boys began to chase it, throwing sticks and stones at it, making it squeal.

'Drive it back against the hedge,' cried Elric, 'then we can corner it and catch it. I'll tie it up in my tunic.'

There was no difficulty in the first part. The pigling turned and ran from them, back towards the hedge. But the next moment it had disappeared.

'There must be a hole in the hedge,' said Duri. They searched along, and presently they found it. There was a gap that ran crookedly through the hedge, low down and hard to see because it came out behind a hut on the other side, which shielded it from view.

Duri began to scramble through. He found there was enough room. Elred went and brought Hildis, and they all four crawled through the hedge and out from behind the hut into the courtyard. The pig they had first seen was still asleep on the far side of the yard. She was a big sow. They went across carefully, looking about them to see if there were others, and then as they drew near the wild sow started up from her sleep with a squeal, and ran away towards the hall door, which was ajar. At once a great din of squealing broke out from within, and pigs young and old ran out in all directions. It was a herd of wild pigs that had roamed from the forest and taken shelter in the deserted buildings. They now gathered together in a grunting crowd, the old sows seeming to stand guard over the squealing piglings, between the children and the gap through which they had entered the yard. There they made a stand. Then quickly Elric cried:

'Run quickly!'

The others looked and saw what he had seen. A huge and savage boar had come from one of the buildings behind them and was standing no more than twelve paces away. Disturbed and angry at the alarm of his herd, he was preparing to charge the intruders.

A half-ruined hut was near them. Duri pushed the younger children towards it. Almost at the same moment the boar began his charge, but the children were already round the corner.

'Onto the roof!' Duri said. He pushed Elred up on to a part where the roof-frame was showing through the rotten thatch, so that Elred could take hold. Then he lifted Hildis, and Elred pulled her up with him. By this time the boar had turned and was coming back. Duri ran round the far corner of the hut again. The boar was close with the heavy noise of its charging and the hiss of its breath, and it would have caught Duri and gored him, but that for a moment it turned its head, seeing the legs of Elric in the air above him, for Elric was not yet safely onto the roof. The boar swung his great head and before Elric could draw up his leg the flashing tusk had slashed it. The boar stopped in his tracks and tried again to attack where he had so nearly succeeded, but Elric by now was up, and Duri was climbing onto the roof from the other side.

Hissing and grunting the boar stood below them, looking up, its mouth half-open and slavering, its tusks gleaming like knives. All around the sows and piglings were running and squealing and grunting. Hildis was weeping and screaming with fright and Elred was trying to comfort her, while Elric was binding his bleeding leg with a strip torn from his tunic. Duri had pulled a loose stake of wood out of the roof, to use as a weapon.

'It is growing late,' he said, 'and nobody knows where we are. You three will be safe here on the roof. As soon as these beasts move away I will get down and go back through the hole and run for help.'

But he had to wait a long while for his opportunity. The sun was low and the shadows long on the ground before the boar ceased from grunting round and round the hut, and wandered further away. The other pigs, too, began to go back into the shelter of King Egbert's great hall, and presently Duri said: 'Now I will go. You must stay here. Do not get down. I will not be long.'

He climbed quietly down from the roof carrying his stick and moved round behind the buildings out of sight of the boar, which had settled down and appeared to be sleeping some way off. Duri had not far to cross in the open, and the boar did not stir. The children saw him slip between the hut and the hedge where the hole was. Then after a moment they heard a pig squeal, and the boar lifted his head. They heard Duri laughing from the other side of the hedge. He shouted to them:

'There was an old sow lying right in the hole. I had to prod her with my stick to get her to move. Now stay where you are.'

They heard him run off, and they waited.

Dusk is a terrible time, when the white sky grows red and the green grass becomes black, and the earth is drinking up the last of the day. Through the darkening woods they presently heard the men coming. There were fiery torches. There were dogs barking. There was a horn blowing, there was laughing. Voices shouted: 'Are you there? Are you there?' and the children shouted back. The pigs began to stir and squeal again and to run about in the yard. The great boar was standing, his feet spread apart, showing his teeth and looking from side to side with his little red eyes. The men had arrived at the gate.

As the gate shook and rattled with the men breaking down the fastenings, the pigs began to run in all directions. Some ran for the hole in the hedge, but they were driven back all squealing, for men and dogs were waiting on the other side. Then the gate broke open and the men and dogs and torches and spears came in and lit the darkening yard. They stood and looked a moment before one shouted: 'There he is!'

The boar turned and ran, the men and dogs were after him, along the length of the Dragon Hall. He turned at the end to come down the other side again, but ran into his own herd of sows and pigs, tumbling along the other way, chased by the shouting men. They kicked and struck with their spears and got him into a corner where he turned at bay, and there was a sudden pause, waiting and grunting.

The children were down from the roof. Elred and Elric with his blood-soaked leg, ran at once to join Duri and the other boys where the men were, to watch the killing of the boar; but the men drove them away.

'Little fools out of the way! Back to your mothers!'

So they could not see what went on. They chased an old sow and her piglets into a shed. Prayn, the vill-reeve, put Hildis on his shoulder and with another man to light the way took her homeward through the dark woods. She held onto his head, fearfully listening to the din in the torchlight at the Dragon Hall behind her, where the boar and the men and the dogs, with spear and tusk and fang and fire were fighting out a hard and bloody death.

CHAPTER SIX

The King Invited

FOR some time after the episode of the pigs Hildis would never accompany her brothers to the Dragon Hall; but the boys with others from the vill went there often and made it a place for themselves. Edgar the Atheling joined them. He said: 'This is my place. My great-grandfather King Egbert built it, and it is now mine. But you may stay with me and be my thanes and companions, and I will give you arm-rings of gold, as a lord should do for his thanes.' He made the arm-rings for the time being out of straw.

That summer throughout all Wessex Alfred the King sent to the ealdorman of the shires to collect tribute-money for the Danes. It was a great price he had to pay, to buy peace from them, after a winter and a spring full of hard battles, after his brother Ethelred had died of wounds, and after so many towns and fields and villages had been laid waste. Ethelnoth, ealdorman of Somerset, sent his reeves out into the shire to collect the gold.

The ealdorman's reeve came to Alham at harvest time, accompanied by one of Ethelnoth's thanes and a party of armed men to guard the tribute-money they collected on their way. The Lady Waltruda saw them coming along the river path, and went with Prayn the vill reeve and young Edgar, to meet them among the gathered corn. The shire reeve, when he had been greeted and had refreshed himself in the shade, said that from so large an estate the tribute had been reckoned at sixty gold mancuses. At this Wáltruda cried that she could not find so much money in so short a time, and that the levy was unjust. It was indeed a great price. The reeve said courteously that he would go on his way and return again in a few days for the tribute money, when Waltruda would have had time to collect it.

The next morning early, as the reeve and his party rode away northwards, they met a swarthy, good-looking man on the path above the vill, who stood aside to let them pass. This was Unferth, coming home at last from places far across the sea, where, among other things, he had traded slaves from Africa and Ireland and Cornwall to the heathen emirs of Kurtuba and Tunis. Or so it was said of him, and he did not deny it, though openly he would only say with a grin that he had been a trader in salt. He had lost many teeth and was not handsome when he grinned. Hildis, who had not seen her father before, was afraid of him, and hid behind her mother when this strange man came to the door of the weaving-house, where Waltruda was with her women that day. Waltruda herself hardly recognised him at first.

After the household and his children had greeted him, and after he had sat at the board and Waltruda had waited upon him, which she did as a wife should (though now it went against the grain with her, having ruled the household alone for so long) she asked him what he now intended to do. He answered:

'I have a mind to settle here again. There are going to be changes in this land. You may need me and my friends in the times that are coming.'

'We are paying tribute to your friends already,' said Waltruda. 'Can you do better for us?' She told him of the reeve's visit, and the tribute of sixty mancuses. Unferth laughed.

'You see,' he said, 'the King of Wessex must pay his Dane-money in the end, like all the others. He will not be able to help himself. He is a little man with a book-thing in his hand and a pain in his stomach, like a poor clerk. You have told me so yourself, and others have said the same. The first payment

to the Danes is the beginning of the end. Alfred has made his first payment.'

An old freeman of the vill, who heard this, said: 'The King is a stark battle-leader, stomach-ache or no. It is said he has fought like a lion.'

Unferth mocked: 'It is said. It is said this and that. But what is known is that he pays the tribute money. He is the first of the Kings of Wessex to do so. What more needs to be said?'

Later in Waltruda's bower, where Hildis was sitting on her mother's knee, Unferth came and asked her again how much tribute was demanded for Alham, and when he was told he took a leather bag from his tunic and emptied it out, all gold pieces, onto the board beside her.

'Take this,' he said. 'I will have my stake in this place.'

'It is Edgar's place,' Waltruda answered. 'I can give you no part of it. You know that.'

'You can guide him for me,' said Unferth.

Edgar was not easy to guide, however. Even now, as a boy eleven years old, he had begun to know his value. He knew that Unferth and Waltruda had no authority to rule at the vill except through him, and he knew Waltruda would, because she must, always give him his way in the end. He saw now, at Unferth's home-coming, that Unferth would be likely to do the same.

Edgar came back one evening from the Dragon Hall and said to Waltruda and Unferth:

'My great-grandfather's hall in the woods yonder stands foully neglected. It is kept for cattle and hay, with its roof fallen in. Wild pigs have snouted in it. I wish it to be mended and made fair.'

Waltruda answered that since the new vill was built there had been no need of the old place, and there were no craftsmen to spare for such work, with so much to be done in the vill. Edgar said angrily:

'It is a royal hall of my family. I wish it made fair.'

Then said Unferth quickly: 'You are right, Edgar. It shall be done.' Later, when Edgar had gone, he said to Waltruda: 'It is well the boy should remember his royal kinship. Who are we without this? You are a foreign woman, and I do not even rank as a thane. Moreover, Ealdorman Ethelnoth has no friendship for me in the shire, since I was Eanwulf's man.'

So in the spring the Dragon Hall was made good. The roofs of the hall and some of the other buildings were re-thatched, the walls mended, the dragon-carvings cleaned and gilded, the interior swept and painted, the floor levelled and the hearth rebuilt. Then Unferth began to think how the place might be used.

That year there was a new bishop to be brought to Sherborne, since Bishop Heahmund, old Ealstan's successor, had been slain in battle against the heathen. It was the same battle in which King Ethelred received his mortal wound. King Alfred was now coming to Sherborne for the induction of the new bishop; and Sherborne town, where the King had a great vill and the bishop his abbey, lay not a day's journey from Alham, south of the forest. Waltruda said to Unferth:

'Since the King will be so near, and since King Egbert's Dragon Hall is now so fine again, might not Alfred come here to honour his grandfather's hall, as guest of Edgar? There is good hunting in the forest.'

'I have thought the same,' said Unferth. 'But the hunting is as good at Sherborne. And what if the King refuses? Ethelnoth and the rest would know we were held of small worth.'

'Small worth!' cried Waltruda. 'Edgar is grandson to the Emperor and nephew to the King. You speak like a common fellow, Unferth, to be so afraid of your pride. Besides, King Alfred has known me since he was a child. At the Emperor's court we knew each other. We have played knucklebones together with Queen Judith, travelling along in that waggon, with a great shield across our knees for a table to play on. Refuse to come? Of course he will not refuse!'

'And how often has he come to play knucklebones since then?' said Unferth. 'It is half your lifetime since. However, you may be right.'

Edgar himself went to Sherborne with Waltruda and their company when they heard King Alfred was there at his vill. Unferth, however, would not go. He feared he might find trouble there, if Ethelnoth crossed his path.

Waltruda did not recognize King Alfred when she saw him. She saw a plainly dressed man of middle stature, with a lean face thinly bearded. He was coming along the path from the cabbage garden talking with his gardener, and accompanied by some six or seven of his household thanes, all talking together. He scratched himself under the armpit from time to time, and shrugged under his tunic as though it were uncomfortable. He might have been any ordinary man. But she saw that when he held up his hand all instantly fell silent as for a king, and he stepped forward with a kingly presence, for all his plainness, and greeted them with a smile.

'Lady, you are very welcome. I should not have known you after so long. One should see friends more often, or the secret alterations of time will steal them away bit by bit. And you, kinsman,' he said to Edgar, 'let me look at you. Yes, you have my brother's look, if I remember him rightly. You are doubly welcome.' They moved on along the path together, back towards the houses of the King's place. There were beehives along the side of the path. 'The bees are doing well for us this year,' said the King, 'but, nephew, I advise you to stay out of their way. I had one of them in my tunic this morning, and I am still doing penance for it.'

King Alfred's wife, the Lady Elswitha, had not come with him to Sherborne. She had remained at Winchester, where she was shortly expecting her third child to be born. So, after the King's evening prayers, when they all went to the meal the King invited Waltruda to sit beside him in his lady's place. Edgar sat in the place of honour on the other side of the hall, facing them. After they had eaten and Waltruda had handed the King the napkin to wipe his mouth and hands, she took confidence from the honour shown to her, and asked if for the renewing of old friendship, and for kinship, the King would accept Edgar's hospitality, and come to Alham. The King smiled, but did not at first reply. Later, however, he called to Edgar across the hall: 'Kinsman, is it your wish to have me in your house?' Edgar stood up then, and replied: 'Lord King, it is my wish, if you will.' The King answered: 'Certain things may prevent me, but I will come if I can.'

The new bishop was presented to his people at Sherborne with much splendour, on a fine sunny day, with the priests and monks of the Abbey singing in slow procession, with the golden censers tracing their cloudy pathways of perfume swinging back and forth, with the people from all Somerset, even from distant villages, gathered to see their bishop, and the King and his thanes, pass by along the crowded road to the Abbey church. The King was dressed that day in silks of purple and vermilion, embroidered all over in gold. Gold bands were upon his shoes and leggings, and his crown and cloak-brooch and armlets were all of richly coloured enamel with many jewels.

Ealdorman Ethelnoth was there with his thanes. In the evening, after the ceremony, he went to the King, whom he found sitting on a bench in the open, outside his hall, dictating letters to a scribe.

'King,' said Ethelnoth, 'it is not for me to question your wisdom, but I have a duty to advise you in certain matters.'

'And I have a duty to listen,' said the King. 'But you have no need to beat about the bush, Ethelnoth. What is it?'

'They tell me you have a mind to go to your nephew's house at Alham,' said the ealdorman; 'and I think you should not go.'

The King gave thought to this for a moment, stroking his beard. He had great trust in Ethelnoth. So he said: 'I take it, Ethelnoth, that you have some good reason for this advice?'

'I have no reason that I can well put into words,' said

Ethelnoth. 'But in my heart I have reason. King, I am uneasy. Doubtless these people mean no harm, but they belong to a bad story. They worked no good for your father, nor for mine. I would let them be, if I were you; I would not go.'

'Tush, tush, my friend,' said King Alfred. 'this boy is my nephew, my own brother's son, and he is not responsible for his father's faults, all that time ago. Surely I ought to show kindness. Besides, I have given my word to go if I can. I will consider what you say, but I do not think I can act upon it.'

Nevertheless, in the end, for a quite different reason, the king did not go to Alham at that time. Word came to him from Winchester that the Lady Elswitha had given birth to her baby, a boy, but that the child was ailing and might not live. He therefore decided to go at once to Winchester. He sent for Edgar and Waltruda.

'Kinsman,' he said, 'and you Lady, forgive me this time. I cannot come. But, nephew, I shall send for you to come and live a while at my court, if you will. It is my intention that young noblemen such as you are should be schooled to read and write, and learn Latin. It is the duty of high-born men to have minds trained above the commonness of day to day. Would you, at your young age, come and be one of the first?'

Edgar did not know what to say, and said nothing above a mumble. He and Waltruda next day returned to Alham, where Unferth awaited them.

'Well?' asked Unferth.

'He cannot come yet,' said Waltruda, and gave the reason. But Unferth said:

'Openly, in front of all, he accepted; and then he changed his mind. Ethelnoth must have spoken to him. And the King now takes Edgar away from us, you say. What should Edgar do with Latin? Is this a training for royal blood? Is this a king's business? Or would Alfred make fools of us?'

He bit his lip, and went angrily into the house.

CHAPTER SEVEN

To the Threshold

IT is said that the Devil himself dwells in the north. In the land of Iceland in the northern sea there is a smoking mountain, which is one of the chimneys of Hell. From this black hole Satan comes out to stir up the terrible northmen to do their evil deeds, and to make them worship their false gods, Thor and Odin and Frey. Satan it was who taught them how to build their long, dragon-headed ships, with which to carry his war against Christendom into the farthest corners of God's earth.

So in the south of England in those few years of peace which King Alfred had bought with gold, when people stood and looked northwards they saw that even when the sun was shining in Wessex, the sky to the north was always dark and thick. Along their northern borders there were always heavy clouds, and sometimes from under those clouds travellers returning would tell of the fearful destruction they had seen in Mercia and Northumbria. They told how the northmen had sacked and burnt the holy monastery of Lindisfarne, which had once been, second only to Rome itself, one of the principal treasure-houses of Christian learning, famous throughout the world. Now it was a roofless shell. Sea-birds nested in it. Somewhere among the bleak hills of Northumbria, the travellers said, the godly abbot of Lindisfarne and a small band of his monks were going about from one hiding-place to another, carrying with them in its coffin the body of Saint Cuthbert, their founder. This only they had been able to carry away, to keep it from desecration at the hands of the pagans. Indeed it was seven long years before their wanderings were over, and they were able to return again, with their holy burden, to Lindisfarne.

But here, in Wessex, a year or more after their exile had begun, it was still peace.

Young Edgar went to the King's newly-built house at Winchester, and stayed there many months. Unferth had been unwilling to let him go, but there was nothing he could do to prevent it, the King having bidden him. Unferth feared he would lose his influence with the boy, such as it was. With King Alfred, friend of all his people and hero of all who knew him, this might have been expected. But Edgar was proud and solitary, not ready for friendship. He lodged with some few of the thanes' sons whom King Alfred had brought together to make a school, remembering how Charlemagne, Emperor of the Franks, had founded such a school at his palace of Aix, eighty years before, for the revival of learning. As a boy at the Frankish court with his father, Alfred had seen this school, and talked with the great philosopher John Scotus Erigena there, and it had fired him with a love for learning. But the thanes' sons of Wessex were not of this mood; they were not ready for it. Certainly Edgar was not. He chafed at the long discipline of study, he hated the old master John the Lombard who tried to teach them Latin and writing. He thought it at first merely beneath dignity, and at last little short of contemptible, that the King himself should come, as he sometimes did, and sit in the class with them, and with a fiddlesome pen, dip ink and form his letters. Such work was suitable only for queer people like the King's namesake, Alfred Dane-Leg, the one-legged orphan boy whom the King had fostered and befriended. But it was not for Edgar. He chafed also at the long prayers which the boys attended with the King and his family each day in the King's chapel-house. There had not been much praying at Alham, except at the times for the blessing of fields and cattle for their fertility, or to keep away evil spirits. Edgar saw, too, that his royal blood counted for little at the King's court, where the King's own children were. He chafed to be back at Alham, where his worth was held in more esteem.

While Edgar was at Winchester a royal visitor came there, on his way to Rome. This was Burgred, once King of Mercia, now king of nothing but the money-bags he had been able to smuggle away with him. The heathen had had enough of him, had divided all his kingdom among themselves, and had sent him packing. He would not have got away with his life if they had thought him worth killing.

At harvest-time Edgar returned to Alham and told Unferth what had happened to King Burgred. 'The same thing will happen in Wessex,' said Unferth. 'If you are wise, my young lord, you will make your preparations in the right quarter. I still have friends in Mercia who have lost nothing by all these changes.'

Then Edgar said: 'I care nothing for your friends in Mercia, Unferth. I have friends in Flanders, I believe. Take me to my mother, at Count Baldwin's court.'

So Edgar and Unferth travelled to Flanders, and found the Lady Judith, who had grown very fat, at the Count's castle at Breda, with her many children. The Count also was there. He received Edgar coldly. He cared little for any of his own children, and nothing at all for Judith's child by her former husband. But Judith fussed over Edgar and made much of him and wanted him with her wherever she went; and for a while he liked it. Then he began to find it tiresome. He had hoped to get from her more than this, something to confirm and support the pride of blood which Waltruda and Unferth had always encouraged in him; instead, he found that to his mother he was little more than a new pet puppy, and to his stepfather, a nuisance. His journey was in vain, he would get nothing by it, it would not even be noticed if he stayed or went. He wept from mingled grief and anger. Unferth was as disappointed as he, though he had never expected so much. They returned empty-handed to England, to Alham Vill, to that far corner of Selwood Forest where alone Edgar belonged.

'Best settle here now, and make the most of it,' said Waltruda to Unferth. 'We have everything we need and no one troubles us. Why seek out trouble, then? Best keep out of the way.'

'Trouble is coming soon enough, whether we look for it or not,' replied Unferth. 'We came along by the Mercian border and have heard what is happening there. When the heathen come down upon Wessex again we may have a hard time of it.'

'You blow hot one moment, cold the next,' Waltruda said. 'You have always said we have nothing to fear from the heathen. Where are these friends of yours?'

Unferth shrugged. 'I hope I have some. One can never be sure. Only one thing I am sure of. This time when the heathen come, the days of Schoolmaster Alfred will be over. Let him try teaching his Latin to the Danes. It will be a poor look-out for us all.'

So much for Unferth, who could be sure of nothing. The Viking armies were gathering, it was true, in such force as had never been seen before. From all over the stony, hard northlands, from Gotland and Jutland and Rogaland, from the frozen lakes of Finland, from Stavanger and the Trond, where the bleak sun shines all night long without warmth; from Iceland under the Devil's chimney; from Ireland and Greenland and the coasts of France which they had plundered for so long, and back from the distant rivers of Muscovy they came in their black and golden ships, to have a share in the final downfall and plunder of Wessex. But when the day came at last when the black clouds on the northern horizons of Wessex at last broke open and the barbarous pagan host, commanded by four great kings, came down with their sharp axes to fell the last kingdom of England, things turned out very differently from what Unferth or any other man in his heart expected – except perhaps King Alfred. King Alfred then raised his hand and the army of Wessex took the field. A whole summer long he held the heathen at arm's length in the town of Wareham, where they got nothing for their pains but hunger, sickness and frustration. How King Alfred did this is told elsewhere. Here we have to tell of what came after. It is enough to say that of the four heathen kings, two, Amund and Osketil, were glad at the summer's end to make peace with King Alfred on his own terms, and go away without any gain. The third, King Hubba Yellow-Beard, having put to sea with all his ships, was smitten by God with a great storm which utterly destroyed his fleet upon the rocky coast of Dorset. King Hubba himself escaped, but they say that five thousand men were drowned on that coast, and to this day the fishermen there sometimes drag up in their nets old helmets, shield-irons and axe-heads, all crusted with sea-shells.

The last of the four kings was Guthorm. He, with four hundred men, had ridden and seized the town of Exeter. Here he awaited reinforcements, but it was these who now lay rolling back and forth on the deep sea bottom, under the Dorset cliffs. Too late he learned the bad news, that his luck was out. The army of the West Saxons stood all round him now, in their strength. From behind his palisade, looking out, Guthorm saw King Alfred on a white horse riding through the camp with his thanes, not far away.

'That man there,' said Guthorm, to Olaf Skald, my grandfather, who stood at his elbow, 'that man, King Alfred yonder, has all along been too lightly valued by our people, all except me. But I know his value. I do not underrate him; and I swear by the Earth-Tree that if ever I get out of here alive King Alfred shall have me alone to reckon with next time. And that reckoning, he will find, will be a very different thing from this.'

From any other mouth such words would have been a worthless boast. But Guthorm, like King Alfred, was not a man to be underrated. He planned no path he could not follow. Thus we have come to the threshold of strange and great events.

CHAPTER EIGHT

Matters of Luck and Mercy

IN the war-camp at Exeter King Alfred and the leaders of his army held council. Three ealdormen were there, Ethelnoth of Somerset, Alfgar of Dorset, and the fierce Odda of Devonshire. Odda would have had no mercy on the heathen besieged in Exeter. He stood with his bare knife in his hand, and said with this he would himself gladly cut the throats of every one of them, and flay their skins, and hang the skins to dry, one on every church door in Wessex. King Alfred would not listen to such things. He said:

'Odda, there are four hundred of them there. It is a small number against such forces as we have now. They could not win a battle against us. But if we make them desperate they will fight to the death, as you yourself would do in their place. Many good men of ours would die, killing them. Is this needful?'

'It is very needful,' said Odda. 'Let the heathen be slain, every one of them.'

'Rather, let them starve,' said Alfgar. 'Truly, I fear no battle-wounds; but King Alfred is right. Why should we spend our blood for this? It is not needed.'

'To starve them we must all sit here and wait, like crows on a fence,' said Odda. 'Let us kill them with our hands, and go home.'

So opinion was divided among the war-leaders, though for a time most seemed to favour Odda's way. But the king was still against it. He said:

'Thanes and chieftains of Wessex, if we slay these four hundred, what good will it do us? There are ten times as many more in the north, eager and ready to take their places. Bloodshed in mere anger will create only anger and bloodshed in return. We should gain nothing; but something we might now gain if we show mercy. Let them go back to their fellows in the north. Let them say that we in Wessex can afford to be generous because we are a strong nation and cannot be conquered.'

The King had his way in the end. It was agreed that Guthorm and his men should be sent packing out of Wessex, giving their oath never to return. But not all the lords were easy about it. The fierce Odda sat silently with scowling eyes, his sword across his lap. And in the evening Athelheah, the bishop of Sherborne, came to the King's tent after prayers.

'King Alfred,' he said, 'your words were fair enough this afternoon, but still I doubt your wisdom. I bid you remember the scriptures, how the Lord God sent King Saul to slay the Amalekites. They were to be slain and utterly destroyed, root and branch, every one of them, the Lord said. Yet Saul disobeyed, and spared the life of their king Agag. For this one act of mercy the Lord punished Saul, and took away his kingdom from him. The Lord God is not merciful to his enemies. Should you be more merciful than He?'

King Alfred answered: 'Bishop, how can I say this without seeming proud? I must trust what God has put into my own heart.'

But the bishop persisted: 'Let Guthorm alone die, then, though you spare the others.'

'How could this be?' demanded Alfred. 'Do you suppose the heathen would hand over their king to be slain, without a battle? Would my people surrender me in such a fashion? No; and neither will his. I should look foolish to demand it of them.'

The King spoke irritably, which was unusual. He checked himself, and then said, more gently:

'Lord bishop, forgive me for speaking so. I have a turn of

Odda.

my old sickness coming on me, and it touches my temper. But I will think about what you say.'

When the bishop had gone the King lay down on his bed, and was unable to rise again for two days. His body ached and his blood ran by turns hot and cold in his veins. He vomited often. The vision of his eyes was confused, and his head throbbed so that he could not endure the slightest noise nor the slightest footfall near him. Then on the third morning the fit had passed and he was able to eat again, though he still shivered. This was the usual course of his sickness. While it lasted he lay like one dead.

He did not change his mind about the treatment of the heathen army. In due course, therefore, arrangements were made for them to muster and march northwards out of Wessex. They looked a poor crew, ragged and starved, as they came out of the gate at Exeter. Each of them threw down his shield as he came out, leaving it as a trophy for the Saxons. The besieged men had eaten nearly all their horses. The few that were left were so starved they could hardly carry the baggage that was put on them. Only Guthorm's horse was fit to ride, and on its back he sat proudly, looking around out of his small eyes under the red eye-brows, judging the worth of the Saxon ranks as he rode between them, thinking scorn of them. Truly it might have been better, seeing what came later, if Odda and the bishop had had their way.

King Alfred himself with a strong bodyguard, and Ethelnoth with the men of Somerset, went along with Guthorm for part of the way. He did so, not so much because he feared that Guthorm would turn aside, as that the vengeful Saxons might band together and massacre the heathen along the way, in the treacherous bogs of the great Somerset marsh or among the dark thickets of Selwood. He meant to keep his word, and see it kept by others.

They went by the old Roman road through Ilchester and north towards the Mendip hills. Selwood lay upon their right, the Marsh upon their left. King Alfred rode at King Guthorm's side. For much of the way Guthorm was silent, dwelling in his dark mood, but after a time, looking around him at the wild nature of the land he said:

'Here they might have done it, might they not, King Alfred? I have heard it said that you are wise. Was it wise to let us go like this? Are we not dangerous still? Are we not thieves and killers, all and every one of us? Yet you let us go free, though you might easily have slain us all. Men will tell you we would have been better dead.'

'They have said so already,' answered the King 'and I have replied that I see no virtue in fighting for fighting's sake, or in killing for killing's sake. You have failed, and now you are departing. That is enough for me. I do not seek your blood.'

'By my sword, I would almost rather you had,' said Guthorm bitterly. 'It does not heal my loss of pride, simply to know that all my blood is still in my veins. We of the north think that to die fighting is the best thing that can happen to a man. The blood-red battlefield is the road to Valhalla, where the dead warrior lives again, crowned forever in the glory of his battle deeds. This is why our young men seek battle so eagerly and why they rejoice to kill and be killed. This is what has made us strong. This in the end will make us master of the world.'

'And when you have mastered the world, what will you do with it?' asked King Alfred. 'Will you not live in it in peace, and enjoy the fruits of it, while you can? Or is Valhalla all you fight for?'

Guthorm did not reply. These words made him angry. He felt that Alfred had tricked him by a clever speech without real meaning. He suspected that whatever success Alfred had was due to a fortunate gift of trickery, and nothing more. After a while he said:

'King of Wessex, do not boast that you and your Saxons have defeated us. All last year, not once did you show yourselves on the battlefield. You lay like a fox in the bush, and dared not come out. In the end it was not you who defeated us, but a mere trick of the weather, an unforeseeable storm which wrecked our ships and did your work for you, without you or any man lifting a finger. It was not your wisdom in council nor bravery in the field that saved you. It was merely your luck.'

'Luck we did have, it cannot be denied,' said Alfred. 'But luck is like seed. It thrives best where the ground has been well prepared to receive it. If we of Wessex had not been lucky this time, we were prepared to go on working till the next. Of that I assure you. What else can I say, except that I am grateful for God's mercy.'

'God's mercy!' exclaimed Guthorm. 'What can that mean? The gods are not merciful. King Alfred, I do not understand this kind of religion.'

'Guthorm, if ever you come into my land again I will myself instruct you in it,' replied the King.

Guthorm smiled grimly, showing his teeth, but he said no more, and they rode on in silence.

The Roman road going north into the Mendips meets another that crosses it east and west upon a ridge called Beacon Hill. Here at the crossroads they halted, and King Alfred took his leave of Guthorm. The West Saxon fighting men, gathered under the banners of the King and the ealdorman, sat down on the hillside in the spring sunshine and watched their enemies drift away northwards, like the passing away of winter clouds. Guthorm, with hardly a word, turned his back upon the Saxons and rode off along the grassy track. The four hundred Danes followed after him in a straggling fashion. The Saxons watched them from the hill till they were all out of sight among the distant trees. Then the Saxon contingents began to part on their different ways. As they were making ready, King Alfred saw a hawking party on horseback, who had come along the eastward road and stopped a little way off, seeing all the shields and the banners. The King sent Bracwealla, his armour-bearer, to ask where they came from and what places were near at hand. This part of the country was out of the way, and Ethelnoth had said he did not know the landowners here. Alfred was surprised at this, it being Ethelnoth's shire. Bracwealla returned and said:

'Lord King, these are people from your nephew Edgar's household at Alham. They say it is the only great vill in these parts. It lies a few miles off, down the road.'

'Ethelnoth,' said the King, 'did you not know this?'

'Yes lord,' said Ethelnoth, 'I knew it, but I thought nothing of it. If we go the other way we could be at Glastonbury before nightfall. That would be better, in my view.'

'Ethelnoth, you know I have given my word to visit my nephew's house at some time,' said the King. 'What better time could there be than now? Let us send ahead and ask hospitality for this one night. We need take only a small company. Bracwealla, who is the leader of their party? Bring him here.'

'Lord King,' said Ethelnoth, while the armour-bearer was away, 'I understand why you must go to Alham, though I wish you would not. But in my case I think it would be unwise for me to go. Unferth still harbours the old grudge against me and my family, and I would not wish to have any quarrel show itself in your presence. Take men you can trust with you, but it will be best if I am not among them.'

'Since it is you who say so, I must respect it,' said the King. 'Do as you wish, Ethelnoth. But I shall go to Alham and make good my promise.'

The leaders of the hawking party were Prayn the vill-reeve, and young Elric, Hildis' brother. They came to the King gladly. They said there was meat and mead enough at Alham for the King and all his company. They rode off in haste, with high hearts, to warn the Lady Waltruda of the King's coming, leaving one of their number with the King to guide him to the vill.

CHAPTER NINE

A Promise Given

THE king took with him Bracwealla the armour-bearer, Ulfstan his herald, his mass-priest, and a bodyguard of forty men of his following, commanded by an old King's-thane whose name was Britnoth. This Britnoth was tough and scarred like the bark of an oak-tree, hardened by many battles in his long life, as the oak is hardened by the storm. Britnoth it was whose son had been slain the previous year, fighting alone against more than a score of the heathen at Wareham. When Britnoth was told of this he had not bowed his head nor shown any other sign of grief, but only stood like an oak-tree, rooted in the place where he was when the news was brought to him, not moving a muscle nor saying a word for a long time, till at last the King himself came out to him and took him by the arm. Then Britnoth said only: 'So let it happen to me in the same way, and soon. I have lived long enough.' He went with the King and nobody heard him speak his son's name again. His son was Wulfhere, who had been King Alfred's shield-bearer.

There also went with the King to Alham the young secretary, his namesake, Alfred the One-Legged, who had had his wooden leg fitted with a hook to take the stirrup, so that he could ride with the King on his journeys.

They rode eastward about four miles along the Roman way, to a place where it was joined by a track going south along high ground at the edge of the forest. The guide led them on to this road. They followed it at first through trees, and then through open fields on the hilltop, and then to a steep descent. From here they looked down into the valley of Alham, and saw the wide fields and clustered houses of the vill, with the welcome smoke of hearth-fires rising from the vents in the roofs. A man on the hillside who had been sent to watch for the King was blowing loudly on his horn, and the people of the vill were gathering in a crowd outside the gate. The roadway was yellow with fresh straw which had been put down over the mud, especially at the gateway where the cattle had trodden deep after the wet winter. The people knelt down by the strewn road as the King's banner drew near. From the gateway the Lady Waltruda came out, with her children. Edgar was at her side, but not Unferth. Edgar carried the mead-horn for house-welcome to the King. King Alfred dismounted and took the horn. Edgar drank it first, as was customary, and then the King. Then Waltruda spoke her greeting and presented her children to the King. Hildis had a posy of primroses which she offered to him. She wore a saffron coloured gown with an embroidered girdle. She was a pretty child, now in her tenth year.

In the great court-yard of the vill the hurried preparations for the King's arrival were still unfinished as he and his company passed through to the great hall. Though it was Lent and a lean time of year they had killed two oxen for the feast, and the carcasses were still being cleaned and jointed in the yard. The fires were bright and hot for the roasting. Serfs were loading a cart with fresh straw and bedding to take up to the woods, to the Dragon Hall, where the King and his following were to sleep, though they would feast in the great hall of the vill, the same which Ethelbalt had built for Queen Judith.

At the feast there were more torches burning in that hall than had ever been seen there since King Ethelbalt's time. The rich tapestries which had been embroidered for him had been brought out and hung all round. They had not seen the torchlight or a King's feast since his day.

Hildis watched from the door of the woman's bower, where she had been sent to stay out of the way, with the younger children. Her brothers had been allowed to go into the hall, since they were boys and old enough now to serve at the King's table. But a young girl could not be allowed to go. She could only see from a distance the firelight glowing brightly on the hall gables and the torchlight shining from the high gable windows, over the fence that separated the women's enclosure from the great yard. She heard the noise of singing and laughing as the night grew late and the King's men grew merry, and she was ready to weep for disappointment at being kept away; presently most of the women who had been at the feast came back to the bower, and they brought some meat for the children, which the King had ordered to be sent. In the hush that fell when the harp-singers began their songs in the distant hall she fell asleep.

Waltruda sat at the King's table, as before. Edgar sat with them. He was now seventeen and good-looking like his father Ethelbalt, but of a petulant nature, without grace. He seemed unsure of himself in the king's presence, and the King, noticing this, spoke to him often, to put him at ease. The King asked him where his foster-father Unferth was; 'For,' said he, 'though I have often heard speak of him I have never yet met with him.' Waltruda, not Edgar answered. She said quickly:

'Lord King, excuse him yet again. Had he known you were coming, he would not for anything have been away. But a certain business took him from here three days ago.'

'The business is, Lord King, that I am to be married,' said Edgar.

'Lord, this is not yet certain,' said Waltruda, 'but Edgar is seventeen and there is a wealthy man with great lands between Cirencester and Chippenham, whom my husband Unferth knows; and this man has a daughter. If a marriage can be arranged she should bring a fine bride-price to Edgar. Unferth has gone north to see if an agreement can be made. Needless to say, Lord King,' she added hurriedly, 'nothing would be done in such a matter without your consent.'

'I will gladly give it,' said the King 'if the match pleases Edgar, and if the girl's family is suitable to his rank.'

'They are kin to the Kings of Mercia,' said Edgar. 'I would not marry into base blood.'

Waltruda said that the girl's father was called Agg the Sightless. He had gone blind early in life, but governed his estates as well as most men who still had their sight. He was well known in the border country between Mercia and Wiltshire.

'He must have kept all his wits about him, that's certain,' said Ulfstan, who was near at hand and had overheard this, 'for many a man with his eyesight has lost all his lands to the Danes in those parts, recently. Edgar would do better to marry a bride from Wessex, in my opinion.'

If the king thought the same he did not say so, and the talk passed to other matters.

The next morning Hildis awoke early and crept out of doors into the shadowy world that the few first wakers have to themselves before dawn. The household men were still asleep, on the floor around the hearth, and on the benches. She went out into the vill and across the brook, and up the hill towards the Dragon Hall, where the king and his company slept. She wandered among the trees as it grew lighter, and she heard men stirring in the yard beyond. She did not like to go near, but soon she saw a young man come out. He had a bucket in his free hand, and he walked with a crutch. She saw that he was young Alfred, the secretary. He came towards her on the way down to the stream, and he saw her. For something to say she asked if she could help him with the bucket. He laughed and said: 'Do you think I cannot manage it? You are right, it is awkward, with only one leg. Come along and help me.'

Down at the stream he washed his face. Hildis held the towel for him. Then she filled the bucket and they began to carry it by turns up the hill. Presently she said: 'Now that I have helped you with the bucket, will you take me to where I can see the King?'

'You can help me carry the water to him', said the secretary. 'This is his bucket.'

'But,' she asked with surprise, 'does the King wash himself in a bucket?'

'At his palace at Winchester he washes in a basin of gold,' said the secretary; 'and at Canterbury when he goes to visit the Archbishop, there is a basin of marble; and at his royal vill at Wantage he has a great basin of silver with figures of men and animals modelled all round it. But for the last many months he has been with his army, living in a tent and washing in a bucket. He does as others do. But in return he expects others to do as he does, and that is more difficult.

'Why is it difficult? Because he is a king?'

'Not so much because of that, as because he is not like other men. He sees things differently. It is hard to explain. We who work with him learn many things we would not learn otherwise.'

At this moment they saw two men coming down the path towards them, among the trees. The first was bare-headed, and wore a long plain grey woollen gown almost down to the ground. 'It is the King', said the secretary. The other was the robe-thane, his personal attendant, called Cnebba.

'Namesake,' said the King, as they drew near him, 'what are you doing? Give the bucket to Cnebba here. I thank you for your care of me, but this is not your task, and you know you cannot do it properly. Who is your helper?' And when Alfred the secretary replied that he did not know, the King said: 'I think I know, however. You are the girl who gave me the primroses, are you not?' he said, turning to the girl. 'Your name is Hilda.'

'Hildis, my lord,' she said, and the King smiled. 'I am corrected, ' he said, 'and what are you doing here, Hildis, so early in the morning?'

'I came to have a sight of you, my lord,' she said. 'I could not see you at the feast last night. My brothers saw you, but I was not allowed to go with them.'

'And rightly,' said the King, smiling. 'You are too young for feasts at night. But perhaps you are not too young at breakfast-time. After I have heard Mass you may wait upon me at table, and bring me my ale-cup and my bread. You shall tell me about your life, and what you have learnt in your few years of it. Will that satisfy you?'

'Indeed, my lord,' she said. So they went again towards the Dragon Hall, which now stood among black stripes of shadow from the low and brilliant sunshine of early morning, shining through the trees. The King went to his own place to wash and dress and hear Mass. Then he called for his breakfast, and Hildis waited at his table and gave him his ale-cup, and answered his many questions. And afterwards she went down through the woods to Alham Vill in the bright spring morning, very happily.

The King and his company departed that afternoon, to rejoin Ethelnoth on the road to Glastonbury. But before he left he remembered to thank Waltruda again, and warmly, for the two oxen that had been killed for the feast; for he knew that any oxen remaining alive at this time of the year were needed for work in the fields and could hardly be spared for meat.

'When I come next time I will go hunting here in the forest as my grandfather Egbert used, and I will provide my own meat,' he said.

'We will provide all, and gladly, my lord,' Waltruda said, and she added, on a sudden thought: 'If you will come again, my lord, I can name a good occasion,'

The King bade her name it.

'Edgar's marriage-feast, my lord, if you would honour it.'

'Send and tell me when it is to be,' said King Alfred, 'and I will come.'

Some days later Unferth returned to Alham. He had made a favourable settlement for the marriage of Edgar with the daughter of Agg the Sightless. Indeed, the blind man had been more than ready to make an alliance in Wessex, which he thought might in the end be a safer place for him than where he now was. The heathen had set up a traitor thane to be King of

Mercia, now that Burgred had been driven out. His name was Ceolwulf, and no man's lands were safe from the prowling heathen, with only false Ceolwulf to guard them. Agg had given Unferth a personal gift of money, to buy his favour. Thus Unferth, by degrees, and by one means or another, was becoming rich.

Waltruda told him that King Alfred had promised to come to Edgar's wedding feast, and Unferth at once began to plan how he might turn the event to advantage. Waltruda sent word to the King that the marriage-feast would take place at Alham at the New Year. The King, she knew, would keep his promise.

CHAPTER TEN

Guthorm

GUTHORM the Dane, humped on his horse's back, glaring angrily ahead of him with narrowed eyes under his red brows, rode on with loose rein at an ambling pace down the Roman track which led out of Wessex into Mercia. Following him, straggling out for half a mile along the road, came the four hundred warriors who were all that were left of his kingdom, such as it had ever been, and with whom for a whole winter he had held Exeter, all to no purpose. They were glad to get away with their lives. On the now distant hillside behind them King Alfred and his Saxons stood watching them till they were at last out of sight. The Danes did not look back.

They camped for the night in the hills near Bath, posting sentries in case the Saxons should after all attack them by surprise. But none came near.

Guthorm sat by his campfire, his red beard ruddier in the glow. His chief men were with him. There were, among the others, Asbiorn and Sigurd, two who had been with Guthorm since the beginning, when he first had his own ship. There was Olaf Skald, with his son Skafti, a youth of sixteen. There was Einar Einarsson, whose allegiance Guthorm could not now be sure of; he had a strong troop of his own followers, in Guthorm's force, and might now decide to take them elsewhere. And there was Torgils Auk, a man whom Guthorm thought cunning and reliable, and whom he trusted, though without much liking. This Torgils had an old injury to his leg which he had got at the battle of Ashdown, years before, and the march on foot from Exeter had tired him, so that he had begun to limp. Guthorm had noticed this, and made a wry joke about it while they were eating round the fire. But Torgils answered hotly:

'We are still eating horse-meat here, Guthorm, as we have done ever since Exeter. That is why I am limping on foot, instead of riding. It is not shameful to have to walk, whoever one may be.'

Guthorm replied, angrily: 'What do you mean, Torgils? Do you mean that I should not ride my horse?'

'You are King here,' Torgils answered, 'and you know best what you should do. But even a king may be advised by his friends. Guthorm, let us face matters. We are in a poor state here. Alfred of Wessex has for the second time put a failure upon us. Learn from him. He is a king who would not ride his horse when his friends go on foot.'

'By the gods, Torgils, you should watch your tongue!' Guthorm exclaimed, his wrath rising; but Einar here broke in:

'Peace, Guthorm! Torgils spoke rashly, but he is not a fool, and there is much in what he says. At least if we must learn from King Alfred, let us learn this: that if we keep together and keep our heads we shall be ready to take advantage of better fortune when it comes to us, as it has now come to him. He has had his bad times.'

'All this about Alfred!' said Guthorm, angrily still, though his anger was now less hot, for it seemed to him that after all he could count on Einar's loyalty. 'I have had enough of Alfred for one day,' he went on. 'All along the road I have had to listen to him. How he talks! He twists the words in one's own mouth. He said he would teach me about the mercy of God. His brain must be addled like an egg, to say such things to me. By Odin, if there is any teaching to be done, it is I who will do it! Wessex has not yet heard the last of me. I shall go back there, and when I do, then we shall see who talks about mercy. It will be a very different story then. I swear it, I, Guthorm, before the gods!'

The chiefs nodded and murmured approval of this, though

at the time they had not much faith in Guthorm's words. One of them said:

'The Wessex people had luck on their side. That will change.'

Guthorm then said, speaking almost as if to himself: 'Their luck is Alfred. There are some men born with a special gift of it. Luck follows them, and all who go with them, not for what they do, but simply for what they are. Alfred is one of these; and so long as the Saxons have him for their leader, their luck will hold. So long as they have him.'

'Or' he went on, after a pause, 'so long as they do not lose him.'

The logs of the fire, shifting suddenly, sent up a spear of flame. It glared upon the faces, the weapons, the dark iron coats of the chieftains gathered about. No more was said on this matter. Twenty miles away, at Alham hall, King Alfred was feasting in the torchlight.

CHAPTER ELEVEN

Guthorm's Friends

THEY turned west next day following the river from Bath towards the estuary of the Severn. Rumour went ahead of them through the countryside that a pagan army was on the march. They found farms and villages all deserted at their approach, the terrified villagers having fled with their cattle as fast as they could. So the pagans plundered stores and granaries, and made off with everything they could carry. They began to feel the luck was turning their way again. Late in the day they came to the township of Bristow, which had shut and barred its gate against them. Guthorm sent a herald to the gate, with the message that no harm would come to the town if the people would pay a tribute of food and money immediately; but otherwise he would burn it to the ground. But the town-reeve came onto the platform above the gate and said they were already paying tribute to a viking who, with a fleet of ships, had come in at the mouth of the river two days before, and had promised them his protection against all others; so they had already sent off to their protectors to come and help them, and until these arrived they proposed to keep their gates shut fast. Guthorm at first thought it must be some trick, but he decided to wait, and in due course there did arrive two ships up the river, full of armed men, who sent a spokesman to Guthorm. What the town-reeve had said this man confirmed. The people of the Bristow region were for the present the clients of his master, and Guthorm would have to seek elsewhere for provisions. Guthorm asked who his master was, and the man said:

'His name is Hubba Ragnarsson, Viking; it is not a name to be taken lightly. I advise you to heed my warning.'

Then Guthorm knew that his fortunes were indeed on the mend, and he sent a message to his friend, Hubba, saying he would come to meet him at his camp at Avonmouth. He marched thither with his men next morning, and the people of Bristow unbarred their gates again. However, Hubba's men came back soon after, and took off huge supplies from them for Hubba to sell to Guthorm, on terms very favourable to Hubba; and the Bristow people got nothing out of it but empty bellies.

Guthorm found Hubba an older-looking man and very sour, after the disaster to his fleet the year before. He said to Guthorm:

'I have only twelve ships left, out of one hundred and forty. I used to feast like a king, I had such power. Now I go about like a dog hunting rats. I sniff about along the coast here, whisking up these wretched villages for food. I spent last winter in South Wales. I shall spend next, who knows where? So, now, tell me about yourself. What will you do next?'

Guthorm said: 'I am going to settle my score with Alfred of Wessex, when I have enough men behind me again. But first I have to find them.'

'Do not look to me to back you up,' said Hubba. 'I back nothing now until I know it is already successful. You can play the lion, my friend; I shall be the jackal. As soon as I hear that you are winning victories and have your enemy safely on the ground, I shall come in and get at his throat for you. Not until then.'

'This I should never have believed of you,' said Guthorm. 'Are you not the son of Ragnar Lodbock? Where shall I look for help, if not to you?'

'There are plenty of hungry vikings in this countryside looking for a good leader,' said Hubba. 'Osketil and those others who deserted us last year have done well for themselves. Much land in eastern Mercia belongs to them now. But there are many cast-off companies here in the west, still looking for a good place to settle. If you can promise them any good pickings, they'll follow you soon enough. Go to Gloucester, that's where you'll find them.'

Hubba talked at length about the situation in Mercia. He told about Ceolwulf the traitor, who ruled over the western part of it, by permission of the Danish settlers of the eastern part. 'He will gladly help you, Guthorm,' said Hubba, 'if you can convince him you are prepared to march into Wessex, and will take all the rest of the landless Danes with you, to say nothing of all the other riff-raff who have joined with them. There are runaway slaves, there are Saxons who have been turned out of their lands by the Danes, and are looking for a chance to win something back elsewhere. Wessex land would suit them very well, if they could get it. But you Guthorm, you have already been kicked out twice, what makes you so bold for a third attempt?'

'I told you, I have a score to settle.' said Guthorm. 'I mean to teach King Alfred that all his high talk and his God of Mercy will not help him for long when the unmerciful storm blows on him as it blew last year on you and me. I was not kicked out. I, like you, was cheated by ill-fortune. Next time it will be Alfred's turn for the bad luck. That is what I want to see, almost more than to have his land.'

Guthorm marched to Gloucester and camped there. The whole country thereabouts was overrun with armed bands, Danes and others, just as Hubba had said, who had gathered there during the winter, eating King Ceolwulf's food. Ceolwulf himself came to nearby Cirencester not long after Guthorm had settled his camp at Gloucester, and there held a council of thanes and landowners from the region, to arrange for the feeding of the ever-increasing number of his unwelcome guests. Guthorm himself, with Torgils and a strong guard, went to Cirencester to see what was happening there, and what sort of a man Ceolwulf was.

There is an ancient arena at that place, which is said to have been built by the Romans. It is a circular grassy bank of earth with two entrances on opposite sides leading into the flat central space. Here the meeting was to be held. King Ceolwulf's tent was pitched at one side of the arena, with the tents of the chief men of his guard nearby. There were benches for the principal Saxon thanes and Danish chieftains – for many others had come there besides Guthorm – all forming a hollow square in front of the king's tent and his chair, which was set on a low platform with a canopy over it. The guards and followers of the assembled chiefs could sit on the grass around, or on the steep bank that surrounded the arena. On the top of this bank King Ceolwulf had planted his flag. However, on the morning of the appointed day the weather was wet and stormy. It poured with rain so hard that though the thanes gathered once or twice on the field, they were each time forced to abandon the meeting and take shelter. King Ceolwulf kept to his own house, and sent for those of his visitors whom he considered most important. It was not a large place and there was not room in it for the whole meeting. Those who were left out were crowded into dark huts and under barn-eaves from which the rainwater poured down in streams. Inside the king's house the air was thick and stinking from the steam of wet clothes crowded together, and with all the smoke blowing about from the hearth. The rain came in through the smoke hole in the roof, and the wind through the high windows at the gable-ends. Guthorm pushed his way in with Torgils and two of their men to guard their backs, for Guthorm was not one to leave his back undefended in a crowd of strangers. He thrust through towards where Ceolwulf was sitting with several of his thanes on a bench by the wall. Most of them were dressed in a way suitable to their rank, but there was one, sitting next to Ceolwulf, who was the more noticeable for the dirty drabness of his clothes. He was an elderly man, fat, with an old white woollen cap on his head, a thin fringe of long white hair hanging to his shoulders, and a thin white beard. The rest of him was all in black. He was sitting bolt upright on the bench, looking straight ahead of him, his hands upon his knees. Ceolwulf, at his side, was all smooth and rich. He wore a silk tunic woven with red, yellow and blue stripes, but dark and greasy in places where it seemed he habitually wiped his hands after eating. Now, to pass the time, he was drinking. 'A useful sort of serving-man.' Guthorm said to Torgils afterwards; 'a toothless lion, a snake that has shot his venom, a good dog to bark at the door for his master. If only Alfred were such a man! Or, better still, if only we had such a man in Alfred's place!'

Ceolwulf stood up to greet Guthorm, and made room for him on the bench between the shabby man and himself. The shabby man put out his hands and took hold of Guthorm's arm, moving himself a little aside to make room, but still gazing straight in front of him. 'Where are you, King Ceolwulf, and who is this?' he said, and Guthorm saw then that the man was blind.

'Blind as a bat,' said Ceolwulf, 'but sharp as a needle. He is called Agg the Sightless. He is a man of importance, here, King Guthorm, and he is very wealthy.'

'Not true, not true,' said the blind man; 'Look at me, do I look wealthy?'

'No matter what he looks like,' said Ceolwulf. 'Here, old, bat, take it.' He pushed his arm across in front of Guthorm and put the horn of ale into the blind man's hands. Ceolwulf was a little drunk. 'Drink it down,' he said. 'Do not be anxious. I shall not give the game away. We all know you. You are a great man. He is a great man,' he repeated, this time leaning back and putting his mouth close to Guthorm's ear. 'He has wealth and influence and a young daughter, who is to be married into a family of kings. He will have royal grandsons, no matter what he looks like.'

'She is to marry your son?'

'I am flattered, King Guthorm, that you should think so,' said Ceolwulf. 'He flatters me, old bat, does he not? No, not a son of mine. Of the royal house of Wessex, no less.'

'Enough, have done with it!' said Agg. 'You do me harm, King Ceolwulf. Here, take back the horn.' He started to rise to his feet, but Ceolwulf restrained him, saying no harm was intended. 'Ill will come of it,' said Agg, 'to talk of such things out of season. Do not heed him, King Guthorm. He makes too much of it. It is nothing to do with the royal house now reigning. A young nephew, a nobody, a nobody. Pay no attention.'

'By the body of Saint David, you have drunk it dry,' said Ceolwulf, and held out the horn to be filled again. 'What a sly one you are, old bat. Come now, we are all your friends here. We admire your cunning, old bat. Take it, Guthorm,' he said, pushing the full ale-horn into Guthorm's hands, 'and drink to the marriage.' He once again put his mouth against Guthorm's ear and whispered: 'The boy's father was King of Wessex, Alfred's brother, no less. His mother a Frankish princess, the Emperor's own daughter, no less. No less than royal, both sides, and all for the old bat's grand-children. Drink it down, Guthorm.'

'Pay no attention to him, Guthorm', said blind Agg once more, but Guthorm was attentive to every word.

There was a flash of lightning, which was followed by a loud burst of thunder that put a stop to all talking for a moment, and then hailstones like large pebbles clattered against the walls and pelted in through the smoke-hole. They hissed in the fire, and streams of water ran out from the hearth. In this diversion no more was said about Agg's daughter, and the old man quickly steered the conversation in another direction.

Soon afterwards the rain suddenly ceased, and the sun shone out from the clouds. The men for the assembly came out from the dripping houses and made their way over the pudgy ground to the arena; but here all was a lake of water. It was decided to put off the assembly till the morrow. Guthorm asked Torgils if he had heard what had been said between Ceolwulf and Agg. Torgils said he had heard most of it.

'Say nothing about it,' said Guthorm, 'but find the blind

man. Keep close and make friends with him and his people if you can. I shall return to Ceolwulf.'

Ceolwulf had returned to his drinking. He welcomed Guthorm effusively. Others of the chieftains were there. Guthorm made full use of his opportunity to get on good terms with them. He intended to be recognised as a leader among them. Any rivals for this position he would have to deal with later. So he spent the day winning allies, and when night came, more than half drunk, he at last found himself alone with Ceolwulf, all the others having drunk themselves to sleep on and under the tables.

'Like boys,' said Ceolwulf. 'Babies. Only you and me. Fill up, Guthorm.' So Guthorm filled the ale-horns again, and began to find out what he wanted to know. Before Ceolwulf in his turn joined the sleepers on the floor, Guthorm had heard all the story of King Ethelbalt and his marriage to Judith, and of the birth and upbringing of Edgar. He learned about Unferth, whom King Ceolwulf had known in other years, while Unferth was in Mercia.

'But this Edgar, since he is the eldest son of the eldest son, should not the kingdom be his, by right?' asked Guthorm, presently. 'Is this not the Saxon custom?'

'All other things being equal, it is the custom,' Ceolwulf replied, 'but in time of war other things are often not equal. Strength is strength. Alfred is King. No one questions it.'

'But if Alfred were not King?'

'Strength is strength,' said Ceolwulf. 'It would depend. Edgar might do. Unferth and old blind Agg would like to think so. What is in your mind?'

But Guthorm did not say what was in his mind, and Ceolwulf presently fell asleep. Guthorm then made his way with difficulty to the door, and went out into the clear night. He stood alone in the middle of the hall yard, his head far back, his face upward to the stars. He spoke aloud to the sky.

'So, then, he, that Alfred,' he said, 'he is no better than the

rest of us, after all. I am a viking and a thief, and Ceolwulf is a traitor and a thief, and Alfred too is a thief, for all his great talk. You, King Alfred,' he suddenly shouted aloud, 'you with all your talk! All that of the mercy of God, all that of living in peace, all that about the seeds of luck! Such high talk, and there you sit all the time with your backside planted on another man's chair. I will pull you down out of it! Next time, my sword will do all the talking. Strength is strength! You shall learn!'

It was not true that King Alfred sat unlawfully upon the throne of Wessex. It was not true that young Edgar might at any time have claimed the throne; nor was it likely, even if Alfred were dead, that such a small claim as Edgar then might have would be upheld by the nobles of Wessex. Guthorm knew this. But the rage he had in his heart against King Alfred would take anything for fuel, however false.

CHAPTER TWELVE

A Certain Time and Place

THE sun next day shone down upon the mud, and a wind blew, drying the ground a little. The thanes of English Mercia assembled once more in the arena, and the trumpeter from the rampart top announced the arrival of King Ceolwulf and his councillors, to begin the meeting. He came with muddied cloak, slithering with unsteady foothold among the puddles. His position in the divided kingdom was no less slippery. He had to command what respect he could from his Mercian lords, and then use it to make them pay heavily in food and money to keep their Danish parasites alive, whose camps were spreading and becoming more crowded every month as new arrivals from other parts of England and from overseas came in. These at any time were ready to take what they wanted by force if they were not given some part of it without. Already three villages near Guthorm's camp at Gloucester had been raided, and men, women and children had been carried off and sold as slaves far away in northern Stavanger and southern Spain. Yet in spite of such things as this Ceolwulf was not able, during the first day of the Assembly, to persuade the thanes to pay all the tribute-money which his Danish guests demanded from him. A meeting was called again for the next day, but that evening many of the thanes, especially those who lived in the south near the borders of Wessex, where they may have felt they had some protection, were seen to be leaving for their homes.

Torgils came to Guthorm's tent. 'The blind man is having his horses saddled,' said he. 'He means to be away tonight. I learn that his village is not more than fifteen miles from here, so he will be safe home and his gate barred before midnight.'

'Then we will go with him,' Guthorm said. 'He is of great value to us. I would not have him come to harm upon the road.'

Guthorm now had a plan. Since the moment he had first heard of the Atheling Edgar, his mind had been working upon it. When next he marched against Wessex – and he intended it should be both soon and sudden – he meant to set up another King of Wessex in Alfred's place, a servile, pliable king, one like Ceolwulf, who would serve to divide the loyalties of the Saxon thanes while the Danes divided their lands. And who better to play the part of such a king than this young Edgar? No matter how slight his claim to the throne, it was enough for Guthorm's purpose. For Guthorm now believed that the strength of Wessex lay chiefly in the person of King Alfred himself. This one pale man, notwithstanding all his prayers and his books and his preaching, had stood armed in the ranks of warriors upon the blood-wet battlefield time and again, and by his mere presence there, as Guthorm himself had seen, had caused the iron-bound shield-wall of the Saxons to stand firm against the whole onrush of the heathen, that violent force which, like a tumbling of great rocks down a mountain-side, no army in the world had been able to withstand until Alfred, the pale King of Wessex, had suddenly blocked the way. To strike at Alfred, therefore, by whatever means, to strike at him in person if that were possible, or, if not, to strike at least at his reputation; to pull him down, to stop his mouth, to show him to the world as nothing more than a small, sick, ordinary man without any magic, this alone might do more than any other thing to take the heart out of the men of Wessex and lay them open to the final, brutal truth, that the gods were brutally unmerciful, that the world belonged only to the brutal strength of the strong, and not to Alfred and his kind. Guthorm raged in his heart against Alfred. To pull him down, with everything he stood for, had become for Guthorm almost a sufficient plan in itself; and Edgar the Atheling, he now believed, might be made the instrument of it.

So Guthorm and Torgils saddled their horses and with a small company rode out of the town, following the blind man's path. It was late in the evening when they saw the dark cluster of Agg's horsemen riding ahead of them. Blind Agg, with his sharp ears, was the first to hear the distant hoof-beats of Guthorm's troop following after him upon the road. Not knowing what it might be he was afraid, but his servants, who led him on a rein, told him they were in open country without any hiding-place; so he halted and waited for Guthorm to come up with him. He was not the less uneasy when he learnt who it was. Guthorm assured him that he had nothing to fear. He came in friendship. He, Guthorm, needed help and advice.

'I am a poor man, I have no money,' said Agg. 'What other help can I give?'

'You can help me to make a king in Wessex,' said Guthorm, speaking close against him.

Agg held silence for a space. Then he said: 'I do not know what you mean, Guthorm. But come with me to my house. We cannot talk of such things on the highway.'

So Guthorm followed the blind man in the dark to his great black house near Malmesbury. It was all black with tar on the outside, and black with soot within. Many servants brought torches when they arrived. There was food ready in the hall, for Agg had sent ahead to prepare his coming. Agg's wife was there, a pale grey woman looking like a ghost in that black place; and with her was a little girl, her daughter.

'Is this she, this child?' asked Guthorm.

'Ah, it is as I thought,' said Agg. 'That is why you are here. Yes, this is she.'

In the dark background of soot and shadows, where old smoky tapestries hung between the posts of the hall, Guthorm then saw another figure standing. He had a dark-red tunic and a fine cloak edged with fur, a richly sheathed knife at his belt, and gold armlets upon his right arm, like a thane. Agg's wife said:

Unferth.

'Husband, the lord Unferth is here also. He has good news for us.'

Agg the Sightless fidgeted nervously with his hands, feeling for the table's edge. He bade Guthorm and his company be seated. He called for drink. He did not speak to Unferth, and Unferth seeing Guthorm and the armed men who were with him, drew back into the shadows again. But Guthorm had heard his name and remembered what Ceolwulf had said of him. He said:

'Friend Agg, do not neglect your other guest for my sake. He is your friend and Ceolwulf's. Should he not be mine also?'

So Unferth came forward, and sat with Guthorm and Agg at table in the long dark hall. There they ate, and spoke little. Later, when the meal was finished and the platters carried away, Guthorm said:

'Friend Agg, send all your people out of the hall so that we three can sit and talk alone. There may be good fortune for all of us in this meeting.'

So the hall was cleared. Torgils with Guthorm's men went out at the door, and in the dark night outside they waited, their hands upon their swords. Torgils watched through a chink of the door. Outside the other door at the far end the servants of Agg and Unferth waited also, their spears beside them. Who could be certain, in days like these, that no sort of treachery was intended? It was unwise at any time for a lord to go alone, beyond the reach and protection of his friends. But the treachery of that night was only in the plan which the three men sitting alone by the hearth in the empty hall now began cautiously to feel out between each other, letting out only inch by inch what was in their minds. As the night went on, the few torches burnt out, and only the glowing embers of the hearth gave light enough to show the faces of Unferth and King Guthorm to each other. For Agg the Sightless all faces and all darkness were the same.

They spoke first of Edgar's betrothal; then of his parentage;

then of the kingship of Wessex; then of King Alfred. Guthorm said that if any mischance should come to Alfred, Unferth might think that Edgar would have a claim at least to that part of the kingdom over which his father had once ruled. Unferth replied carefully that it might seem to be so, but that most, if not all of the Saxon lords, would resist it, and give the succession of the whole country to Alfred's children. 'Who would get any advantage, he asked, if Edgar were to attempt the throne?'

'And if the attempt should fail . . . !' said Agg. 'No, no. Unferth, it would be folly. We are very well off as we are.'

'We are fortunate, indeed,' said Unferth. 'Edgar stands in King Alfred's favour, and may gain power and wealth that way. I came here today bringing good news for you. I now have it for certain that the King will come himself, in person, to Edgar's wedding feast. I have not told you of this before. I thought it likely he would change his mind. But he has now sent his under-reeve to Alham to make arrangments for his coming. The reeve was with us three days. He did not go till yesterday noon. Now that all is certain I came at once, myself, to tell you.'

'Since yesterday?' asked Guthorm. 'So this place Alham is not far from here?'

'Not far, with a good horse,' said Unferth. 'It is about forty miles.'

Guthorm was silent again. Agg and Unferth talked of the money needed to entertain the King and his followers at the betrothal feast; but Guthorm was thinking to himself: 'King Alfred will be coming soon, in person, to a certain place not far away from here, and at a certain time that is known beforehand.' He said aloud:

'When do you hold this feast?'

Certainly Unferth at that moment must have suspected the danger there would be to King Alfred in his reply. Certainly at that moment he held back, hesitating to take this step, yet not now knowing how to avoid it. He was silent. But blind Agg spoke for him, out of the darkness.

'It will be in midwinter, on the twelfth day of the feast of Christmas, in the New Year. Is it not so, Unferth?'

Unferth still paused for what seemed a long while before replying. Then he said slowly: 'That is so.'

Guthorm said: 'You will have to provide food and lodging for a great company, will you not? The King will surely not travel without a following.'

Unferth's voice answered slowly out of the dark:

'Surely not. He will bring his guard company, his thanes and servants. Who knows whether many or few? Nothing is certain. They will lodge at King Egbert's great house in the wood. The house is called the Dragon Hall.'

Guthorm said: 'Doubtless the place can be well defended.'

Unferth did not reply, and there they left the matter.

A grey light, the first of morning, began to show in the smoke-hole overhead, and Agg shouted for his serfs to come and put more logs on the fire.

CHAPTER THIRTEEN

The Gods

LATER in the morning Guthorm rode away with his troop. Before he left he unclasped the enamelled brooch that fastened his cloak and gave it to Unferth, saying: 'My camp is at Gloucester. Friends who have news for me are always well rewarded there.'

Unferth stayed till next day at Agg's house; then he mounted and rode back towards Alham. As he rode through the forest paths he said to himself:

'It means nothing. I said nothing to Guthorm that he could not have learned for himself. He would in any case have learned it from Agg. Was it not Agg who spoke first? Besides if Guthorm means to do harm, he has power enough to do it when and wherever he chooses. King Alfred's luck cannot hold for ever. What difference will it make whether he comes to Alham or not? As for me, I have to find my fortune where I can, and young Edgar's fortunes are still the best for me. Meanwhile what harm have I done the King?' But he knew he had fastened his cloak with Guthorm's brooch.

Guthorm as he rode back to Gloucester said to Torgils:

'We shall see Unferth again. In a little while he will make his decision. He will come to Gloucester. We will treat him well. He will be worth more than a thousand men to us.'

On the hill not far from his camp at Gloucester there was a grove of ash trees. This Guthorm had given to the gods. In the middle of the grove he had put three images, of Odin, Thor and Frey. They were the same ones he had set up on the forward lifting of his ship, ten years before, when he had first sailed from Jutland. They were neither large nor well-shaped, being little more in fact than mere stumps of wood with heads and arms, eyes and mouths and noses crudely cut, and runes carved upon their bodies. They stood upon a trestle in the middle of the grove. Before them were three pots of blood, which they had for nourishment, and upon the surrounding trees were hung the carcases of dogs and horses which had been sacrificed to them. Two dead men hung there. Also, all over the trees were nailed bunches of long hair, which the warriors of the heathen army had cut from their heads and dedicated to the gods. The whole sanctuary was surrounded by nine long ropes, fastened from tree to tree with nine knots, forming a triangular space.

Into this grove Guthorm went in the evening, and stood before his gods, who faced him with carved eyes and grimly smiling teeth. He said:

'It is I, Guthorm. So far, it prospers. I thank you; but more is needed. Are you helping?

'The army grows by hundreds daily. But make it grow by thousands. I have already two thousand, three thousand men. I have friends and allies. I will need more, more. Are you helping?

'Time is running away. Do you smell autumn already? Do you smell winter? What blood shall we spill for you in the New Year? Are you helping?

'Listen, mighty lords. Next year you shall feast in Wessex, in Alfred's temple-houses. I myself will place you there, with these hands. Do you hear me? But between now and then you must work for it. Alfred must be made blind and deaf. Make him and his god and his people all easy in their own homes until midwinter, until the New Year. Thereafter if you and I do our work well there will be nothing more they can do. We shall have Alfred by the leg, and it will all be over. Do you hear me? But you must be working. Are you working, great lords?'

He heard the lonely evening wind passing through the leaves. The trees of the grove hissed and swayed, the branches creaked.

The hanging carcases rocked gently in their bonds. The three gods, unmoving, grinned with their teeth and their wooden eyes.

Guthorm left the grove and went down the hill to the trampled camp-ground and the swarming men.

CHAPTER FOURTEEN

A Promise Kept

THAT winter the people of Wessex kept the feast of Christmas in peace in their own homes. King Alfred was with his family at his great new house at Winchester. On Christmas Eve he confessed his sins, and prayed all night in his chapel, keeping watch as he might have done for the birth of his own child. At dawn he dressed himself in his finest clothes, and he and the Lady Elswitha and their children, with Ealdorman Wulfric of Hampshire and all their noble thanes and kinsmen went with great ceremony in procession to the Minster Church where Bishop Tunbeort celebrated the Mass. The high spaces of the Minster were filled with incense and singing. When all was over the people of the congregation kissed each other and prayed God to keep them in peace, and the King feasted with his friends in his great hall there at Winchester.

On the first day of the New Year thereafter King Alfred made ready to go into Somerset where, as he had promised, he was to attend the wedding of his nephew, Edgar the Atheling. The King took only a guard of thirty shield-companions, since at Alham there would be Somerset men to serve and protect him. As the baggage-horses were being loaded in the courtyard there came through the gateway on horseback a man who to most there (but not to all) was a stranger. He was indeed a foreigner, a Frank. He was dressed as a fighting man. He wore a great plain helmet of iron, from within the shadow of which his sharp eyes, his beaked nose and wisps of his iron-grey hair looked out. His sword hung in a huge scabbard. A war axe hung at his saddle bow. He had with him a pack horse on a leading-rein, which showed him to be a traveller from a long journey. Broad, stark and heavy, he dismounted, and asked for the King.

But the King who himself was in the yard at the far side, out of sight, heard him and said: 'I know that voice.' He came forward, and the newcomer saw him and went and bent the knee to him, and then they greeted each other as old friends.

The newcomer was called Guntram. He was a Frankish knight who had fought with the King at Ashdown, and had been his constant shield-guard and battle-companion until some three years since, when he had gone overseas to Rome, and beyond. 'And now, my lord,' he said 'I have returned with gifts for you, and with some news. The news is not all good, but the gifts are something.'

He unstrapped from his horse a bundle wrapped in canvas. He cut the cords of it with his knife, there in the yard, and opened it out. Within was folded a fine cloak of purple-red, embroidered all over with little crosses of gold and silver, and bordered round with an embroidered pattern of vine-branches, intertwined and clustered with grapes. It was lined throughout with fine white marten's fur. It was a royal garment, stiff with its riches. Wrapped within it was an ivory box containing the book of the Gospel of Saint John, most beautifully painted, from the scriptorium of the monastery of Saint Denis; and an engraved gold cup studded with garnets.

'I bring these things to you my lord,' said Guntram 'from the Emperor Charles, now Emperor no longer, pray for his soul. I was among his followers when he died, high up in the mountains, on the way back from Italy to France. These few things here he had with him. The Holy Father, Pope John, in Rome gave them to him. He knew that I was coming here to Wessex, and asked me to give them to you, from Emperor to King. Such things were no longer for him. He lay dying in that poor wooden hut in the high snows, and never saw green fields again.'

King Alfred took the red cloak and put it on. He said: 'I will wear this for him, then. These other treasures I give to

S. WALES
River Severn
MENDIP HILLS
Bristol Channel
Wedmor
Kynwit
Polden Hills
Glast bu
QUANTOCK HILLS
The Marsh
R. Parrett
R. Cary
Athelney
Taunton
R. Tone
Langport
Somer
R. Parrett
Ilches
Part of DEVONSHIRE
North Somerset with Selwood in 878 A.D
To Exeter
0 1 2 3 4 5
Scale in Miles

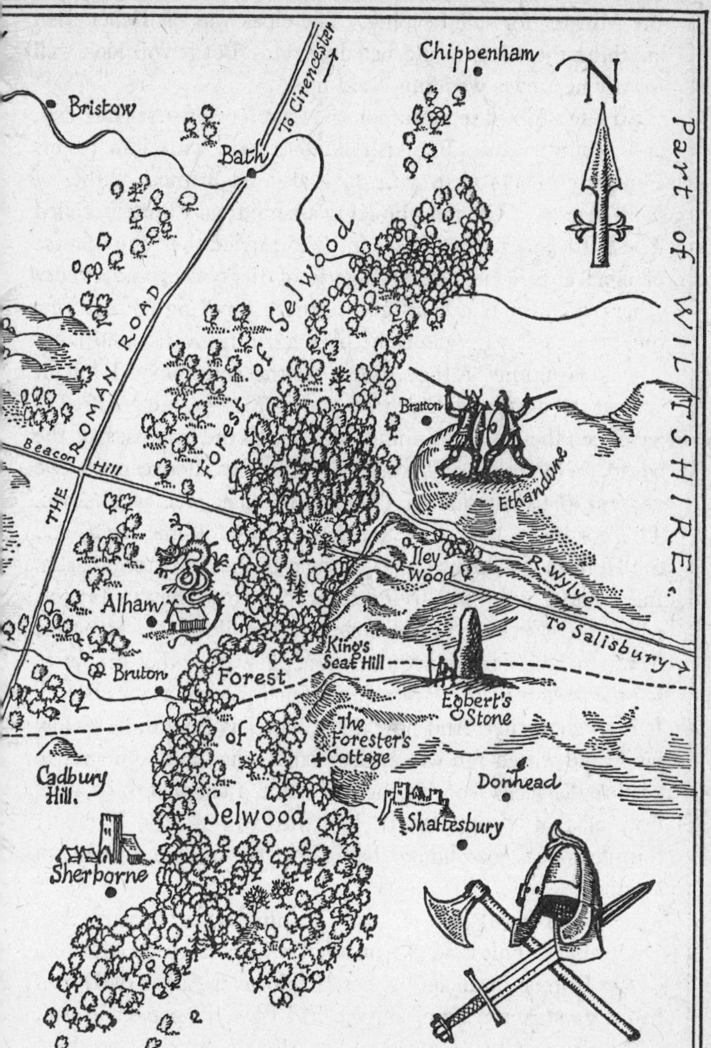

Chippenham
N
Part of WILTSHIRE.
Bristow
To Cirencester
Bath
Forest of Selwood
THE ROMAN ROAD
Beacon Hill
Bratton
Ethandune
Iley Wood
R. Wylye
To Salisbury
Alham
King's Seat Hill
Bruton
Forest
of
Selwood
Egbert's Stone
The Forester's Cottage
Cadbury Hill.
Donhead
Shaftesbury
Sherborne

the Minster for safe keeping.' The cloak was far richer than anything the King would usually wear. 'But it will look well for my nephew's wedding,' said he.

So King Alfred set out upon the road for Somerset that day, and Guntram, the Frankish knight, rode with him in his Company. There were with them also old Britnoth, father of Wulfhere; and Ulfstan, the King's herald; and Bortric, called The Little; and young Escwin, who carried the White Horse banner; and Eclac, son of Sigeric of Berkshire; and twenty others, men of great heart and strength for King Alfred. Few there were of them who came back again from that journey.

Said Guntram as they rode: 'In the years since I fought against the northmen here with you in Wessex, King Alfred, I have seen their swarms plundering in half the countries of the world. In the other half swarm the Saracens. Between the two of them, all Christendom is in more peril than it has ever known. The northmen have threatened the city of Rome itself, and the Holy Father had to send for help to the Emperor Charles. But Charles was busy trying to keep them at bay in France, where the rivers are full of their ships, while at the same time he was making war against his own nephew, the other Emperor, for possession of the River Rhine, or for some such quarrel. It is all confusion. And now that Charles is dead there is only his feeble-witted son whom they call Louis the Stammerer to keep the heavens from falling in France. I am glad to be away from all that, King Alfred. Here with you in little Wessex I can see a clear road and a chance that the bridges will not all collapse.'

It was a hard, cold January evening when they reached Shaftesbury. This is a town on a hill, which had been a fortress of the Britons in ancient times. Ealdorman Alfgar of Dorset had a great house here, and he had come in person to wait at the King's table. He had bed and lodging ready, fires, food and drink. Outside, the horses stamped and broke the crusted ice.

'Lord King,' said Alfgar that evening, 'you know there are some who would rather you did not make this journey. Many remember what happened in your father's time. They feel that the people of Alham are not to be trusted.'

'I know that Ethelnoth thinks ill of it,' replied the King, 'and I respect him, as I do you. But as you see, I do not go without a guard. And what cause have you to think that young Edgar and his people could wish me any harm? Only this old story of years ago, before Edgar was even born. Truly, if we are to nurse old suspicions forever, among even our own kin, we shall finish by being unable to move between one door and the next for fear of the knife. I hope I have no enemies except the heathen; and my reports tell me they show no sign of moving from their winter quarters near Gloucester. It is far enough from here.'

'Have no fear, Alfgar,' said old Britnoth. 'The King is well guarded. We shall not get drunk at this wedding feast.'

From Shaftesbury next morning the King and his party rode thirteen miles north-westwards into Selwood Forest until they came to the bridge at Bruton. Here the Atheling Edgar awaited them, with a party of honour, on good horses and all finely dressed. The lord Unferth was with them. This was the first time Unferth had seen the King. Edgar presented him, and the King took him by the hand. Then the whole party moved on together the last three miles of the way, over the hill and down to Alham in the valley. As they came into view over the hill from Bruton a man of Unferth's, a Welsh slave whose name was Howel, saw them from the place he had been posted, on the opposite hillside above the vill. Howel was a man to whom Unferth had promised freedom for faithful service. He had a horse tethered among the trees there, out of sight. When he saw the King's party in the distance he mounted, and rode away northward as fast as he could. Such was his instruction.

CHAPTER FIFTEEN

Wedding Guests

SO FOR the second time the Lady Waltruda came out to greet the King at Alham Vill, and for the second time Hildis, the house-daughter, welcomed him, not this time with spring flowers but with a branch of mistletoe. As before the King and his company were given royal lodging in the Dragon Hall among the trees. The winter sun blazed upon the gilded dragons high in the gable, and glittered on the frosty roof, over the high black hedge of thorns which enclosed the Hall and its outbuildings all round. The King complimented Edgar upon the splendour of the building, and Edgar then requested to be allowed to guard the King himself that night, which was the last before his wedding. He would have with him a company of the men of Alham to keep watch in the courtyard outside the Hall. It was a courtesy which the host owed to his guest, and the King willingly allowed it; but since they would need the outbuildings of the yard for shelter in such cold weather there would be no room there for the horses of the King's troop, and these therefore were taken and stabled in the vill below.

The young bride had arrived in the vill the day before. Her name was Edith. Her mother Gifu, and her eldest brother whose name was Beorn had come with her. Blind Agg, pleading the difficulties of the journey for one of his age and condition, had stayed at home. Edith and her mother were lodged in a new house which had been built in a meadow between the stream and the great hall of the vill, standing a little on its own. Some of Waltruda's women had been sent to attend them, with Hildis as a companion for Edith who, though she was four years older than Hildis, hardly seemed as much. She was pale and a little frightened at her new position and her new surroundings.

Agg had already paid over the greater portion of his daughter's bride-price. The remainder Beorn had brought with him to be given at the troth-feast that night. The marriage feast was planned for the night following.

At the troth-feast the King sat in the high place on the west side of the hall, with his companions ranged in order on each side of him. On the opposite side sat Unferth and Beorn, with Edgar and Edith, one on either side of them. Hildis and her two brothers were bidden to wait upon Edith and Beorn at the opening of the feast, as was customary. Waltruda waited upon the King. She carried the full drinking horn, mounted with gold and agate, to the King's table.

'Lady,' said the King as she held out the drink to him, 'Your hands are trembling. Are you not well?'

'It is heavy, lord,' she answered. 'I am well. Only the smoke of the fire has got in my throat a little.'

'Drink first, then, and refresh yourself,' said the King. This she did, steadying her hand.

Later that night, after the troth-plighting, and when the last of the bride-price had been handed over, the King made his own gift to the bride, a gold circlet for her head, of fine Lombardy work, engraved, and set with precious stones. The King did not stay late at the feast, since there was to be a deer hunt next morning in the forest, before the wedding feast. He returned with Guntram and Britnoth and the others to the Dragon Hall. Edgar went with him and also Elric and Elred, Hildis' brothers. Unferth and Waltruda took leave of the King for the night at the gateway of the hall-yard.

'What is the matter with you?' said Unferth to Waltruda, when they were alone later. 'You are trembling.'

'It is the cold,' she said. 'Unferth, what is to happen?'

'Nothing, lady,' he said. 'What is in your mind? Go to bed.'

Early next morning Unferth with his hounds and his huntsmen waited for the King in the forest clearing before the Dragon

Hall. He had brought the horses for the King's party. It was a small party that rode that morning. The King had with him only seven or eight of his friends, Escwin and Guntram among them. Unferth said his best huntsmen had been out since the previous day, to drive and harbour the deer in the parts of the forest lying to the north; so northward they rode. Unferth stayed at the King's side. Escwin and Guntram were close at hand. They rode for two or three hours, yet had no sight of any deer. Escwin said jestingly to Unferth.

'Your huntsmen have lost the knack, Unferth. There have been no deer in these parts since King Egbert's day.'

'Soon now,' said Unferth, grimly, not liking this. 'My huntsmen know their game. This way.'

So they rode northward still. Presently they came to a narrow place between high rocks topped with trees. Here Unferth suggested they should rest a while and eat. But at this moment one of the King's men, little Bortric, who was noted for his keen sight and hearing, said he heard deer in the forest a little way off, going south. The King therefore gave the word at once, trusting Bortric, and they followed Bortric's lead till soon, across a clearing, they spied several head of deer at once, running south. They gave chase, and presently shot a hart and a hind. Unferth then was for returning northward, but Guntram said: 'For my part, I would be content with this. It is a long ride back, and there is much to do before this evening's feast.' The King agreed with this, and so they had food and drink there, where they were, at a different place from the gulley which Unferth had suggested, and rode back to Alham in the afternoon.

Old Britnoth had not been with the hunt, but had remained all day at the Dragon Hall. Others of the King's party had gone down to the vill with the men of Edgar's guard. They had found all the people at the vill honest and pleasant, said Brinoth; but he had stayed where he was. He said he had a feeling against the place. 'Perhaps it is nothing but my age and the cold weather,' he said. 'There is this wind from the north, and snow coming. But, King Alfred, I could wish to be away from here.'

'Because of the snow, Britnoth?'

'No, lord. Because I do not like it here. There is something wrong. We should go.'

Escwin said aside, to Guntram: 'Britnoth is right. My feeling is that everything here is in hiding. I cannot explain it; but we should go.'

King Alfred answered Britnoth. 'I, too, feel there is much in what you say, old friend. Tonight is the wedding feast. After that there will be nothing to keep us here. Tomorrow at noon we will leave for Shaftesbury, if that will content you.' He bade Ulfstan make the necessary arrangements. He went then to say his prayers, as he did for a part of every day, and to dress himself for the wedding. He put on a plain white tunic, bordered and collared with a pattern of red and gold, and over this he wore the fine red cloak lined with white fur which Guntram had brought him from the Emperor Charles.

Elric and Elred came with torch-bearers from the vill to escort the King and his men to the feast-hall. There was a little snow falling as they went down the hill. When they arrived at the feast hall Waltruda and Edgar were awaiting them. Edgar was dressed in fine colours for his wedding, and he was already a little drunk. He gave the King welcome and escorted him to the place of honour. Waltruda seemed to be uneasy, and went about as if she were unable to leave her stewards to manage the affairs of the feast on their own. She talked for a while with the King, then went away to find the wedding priest who had come from Bruton, over the hill.

'A mere priest,' Ulfstan said to Britnoth. 'Why, for such a family as Edgar's they should have had the Abbot of Sherborne himself.'

The bride came into the hall with her mother and brother. Hildis also was with her. They came first to the King, who greeted them with all grace. He talked a little with the bride, before he himself led her over to her place beside Edgar. They saw she had been crying. Her eyes were red. Edgar took her from the King's hand and pinched her cheek, laughing. She sat between Edgar and her brother, looking frightened and near to tears.

'Stone of darkness!' exclaimed Guntram, behind his hand, to Ulfstan, his neighbour. 'This, for a wedding, is not half so gay as a funeral I once went to in Pannonia. There everybody was happy, even the dead man. A chieftain he was, and he was lying there on a table in the middle of it all, smiling from ear to ear. The food was good, the drink was good, everybody danced and sang and they burned the house down afterwards, all around him. But this—!'

However, the carvers and servers were now at work cutting up the venison and rabbits and game birds, and the salt pork and beef. The platters came round piled with huge handfuls of it all, and the drinking horns full of mead were soon slippery from rich holding. So Guntram presently said:

'Well, this is better. But there is still a strange thing. Where is Unferth? Is he outside, still waiting? What other wedding guests does he expect?'

CHAPTER SIXTEEN

Rabbit Traps

DURI the falconer's son had helped carry the dishes of bread and meat at the feast, and had helped himself as he went around, and hoped to help himself again later that night. But he had set some rabbit traps two miles away up the valley in the forest, and he knew the miller's two sons knew where they were. He suspected they were not to be trusted. To keep an eye on his affairs, therefore, he decided to go up the valley for an hour and look at his traps, while the miller's sons were at work filling and carrying ale-horns in the hall.

Outside, it was snowing slightly. Duri wrapped his cloak around him, and went quickly towards the valley. But before he was clear of the houses of the vill he saw a man standing in a shadow by a door. He saw, as he came near, that it was the lord Unferth. Unferth said abruptly:

'Who is that? Is it you, Duri? Where are you going?' Duri told him, and Unferth then said: 'You know my bondman, Howel? If you see him, tell him I shall be waiting for him in the hall. Tell him to come to me there, at once. Keep a sharp watch for him, Duri.'

Duri was astonished at the way the lord Unferth said this to him, in a manner seeming to be at the same time so anxious and so fierce. He said he would give Unferth's message if he should see Howel. Then Unferth turned away and went quickly towards the hall. The snow clouds had passed away for a while, and a bright moon was shining. But it was very cold. Duri went quickly up the valley till the trees were close together and the sides of the valley steep and dark. In the quiet stillness he could hear the stream at the valley bottom rippling over its pebbles.

He found the first of his traps, and there was no rabbit in it. He went on.

There was no rabbit in the second trap, and he went on again.

Before he reached the third trap, however, he stopped suddenly to listen. The moon had gone behind a cloud. In the darkness and in the silence he made when he stopped and held his breath, he heard the stream, and then he heard a horse neighing, and then he heard men's voices for an instant, very low, some way off. It was too dark to see anything. He crept forward a little, up the hillside to a place where, if the moon came out, he knew he would be able to see an open space in the valley below the trees. As he reached the place the moon came out, shining brightly, and he clearly saw down. He saw men and horses. He saw helmets and shields glittering in the hard moonlight. He saw spears, he saw dark clusters of armed men, a great number gathered there in the valley among the bushes and the trees. Then the clouds closed over the moon again, and in the darkness he could only see shadowy clusters like bushes slightly moving, dark, armed shapes upon the thin snow on the ground.

He turned, very frightened, and crept away until he felt it was safe for him to walk, then to run as fast as he could, back towards the vill. But almost at once he caught his foot in a bramble, slightly twisting his ankle. It was painful, but not more than he could manage. He stood up again, and after a few yards of limping it became easier. Then just as he was starting to run again he heard a horse galloping behind him.

He was in open ground. The moon came out again. The horse and its rider could be seen clearly, also in the open. Each could see the other. Duri stood still. When the rider came up with him Duri recognized him and called out:

'Howel! Is that you?'

'Who is that?' said Howel. 'Ah, it is Duri, the falconer's son. What are you doing here, Duri?'

'Oh, Howel, Howel. The lord Unferth is asking for you, Howel. Quickly, quickly, ride and tell him, there are enemies! Did you see them, Howel? There are armed men in the valley back there! Did you not see them as you came?'

Howel said: 'What have you seen, Duri?'

'There is an army, Howel! Ride quickly, quickly! I think they are the heathen!'

Howel sat blackly still, high on horseback over Duri's head, a dark shape against the moon-covering cloud above. He said:

'I saw nothing, Duri; you are mad.'

'No, Howel. There is fearful danger. Warn Unferth! I will warn other people. There is the King in the vill. He must be warned! Let me ride behind you. Ride quickly!'

Howel said: 'Up behind me, then. Give me your hand, Duri.'

Duri gave Howel his hand, and Howel held it with his own and brought down his other hand holding a knife, and struck Duri with the knife between the ribs. Duri fell gasping to the ground. Howel dismounted with his knife in his hand and bent over Duri lying there, to make sure of him. He had meant to strike a second blow, but now he found he could not. He had liked Duri. He thought the one blow enough for the purpose. He could have wished the boy might live, but he saw now that he would not. He was lying still, only moaning a little. 'He is surely dying,' said Howel to himself. He wiped the blood from his knife onto the ground, mounted his horse again, and rode off quickly towards the vill where Unferth had awaited him for many hours past.

CHAPTER SEVENTEEN

The Bride

HILDIS at the wedding feast stood against the tapestry behind Edith the bride. It had been Edith's wish to have her near, and since Edith had been weeping all day and unwilling to go to the marriage feast her mother and brother had granted she should be allowed to have her friend with her. Edith had taken comfort in the company of young Hildis. Sitting between Edgar and her brother, under the eye of the King himself across the hall, she tried not to weep again. She whispered to Hildis to fetch her cold water and a napkin, to cool her eyes. Hildis went quickly out and across the snowy yard to the kitchen-house to fetch a bowl. A little snow had drifted against the fence by the gate and she bent and scooped it into the bowl. Rising, she saw the serf Howel in the shadow of the gate.

'Lady,' said he, 'is the lord Unferth in the hall? I beg you to find him quickly and tell him I am here.'

'Why Howel, but you can go in yourself,' Hildis said.

'No lady, I had better stay here. Tell him, but tell him alone, and quickly if you can.'

So Hildis ran back into the hall, where all the noise had suddenly died down. Rotri the smith, the singer and harpist of the vill, now sat at the hearthside with his harp to sing a song for the wedding. He sang a famous tale of magic and heroes. Unferth was standing near the door, so Hildis was able to whisper to him quickly about Howel, and quickly he then went out into the dark.

Edith did not eat, nor did she listen to the song of Rotri the smith; but she dabbed her eyes with the snow-cold napkin and smiled at Hildis. The King watched her from his high seat across the hall, and when the song was over, and he had given the customary gift to the singer, he rose and came over, very splendid in his cloak of majestic red, and spoke cheerfully with her and Edgar. He saw Hildis standing there behind, and spoke to her also. It warmed Hildis' heart that the King himself should have noticed her.

'And now, if the lord Unferth is here', said the King to Waltruda, 'is it not time for us to bless the wedding and drink the bride-cup?'

Unferth had at that moment entered the hall. Shaking the snow from his cloak, he came forward and said: 'I am here and ready, Lord King.'

So then all rose to their feet, and the table was carried away from Edgar's place so that he could stand forward with his bride into the centre of the hall, and their hands were joined and the blessing given by the priest. The horns and cups were filled with the bride-ale, and the King called for the health of Edgar and his young bride, the new Lady of Alham; and all who were there, the King and his company, and all the men of the vill, and the womenfolk who stood by the doorway at the end of the hall, shouted and drank the bridal toast. Edgar drank to his bride and passed her the cup. Edgar was laughing and very unsteady on his feet, for he had no head for drinking and had drunk more than a little already. Edith took the cup, yet could scarcely sip from it. She did not weep, however. She sat, then, with her husband in the place of honour, and the people of Alham came, every family, to do their obedience to her and Prayn the reeve announced the name and station of each as they came forward.

But then suddenly, with the heat, and all the crowds of people, and with a noise ringing in her ears, Edith became cold, her face as pale as parchment, and she fell forward off the bench in a faint. Her mother Gifu and the women came to her. She recovered a little, but then she clung to her mother and began to weep and tremble so pitifully that Gifu said:

'I had best take her back to the bower for a little while. She is tired. She did not sleep all last night.'

Edgar said: 'She should come with me. I will look after her now. Is she not my wife?' But the King quietly said: 'The lady Gifu is right, Edgar. Let Edith rest in her own bower for a while.'

So Gifu and her women took Edith weeping, across the snow back to the bower on the edge of the vill. Hildis went with her. Others would have followed, but Gifu sent them away.

In the hall the King said quietly to Ulfstan: 'Let us go now away back to the Dragon Hall. Do you and Guntram tell my people to come as soon as they can. Meanwhile I will speak to Lady Waltruda.'

He went to Unferth and Waltruda and said:

'I am sorry for your sake to be leaving this good feast so soon, but I think the bride will not return here tonight, and I must be away early tomorrow. I give you thanks for your hospitality.'

He took his leave of Edgar also, and went out with Britnoth and Ulfstan and Guntram and the rest up the moonlit path into the woods to the Dragon Hall. Elric and Elred, Hildis' brothers were eager to go with him, but Unferth held them back.

'Stay here where you are,' he said and held each of them by the wrist.

In the bride's house Edith lay sobbing on her bed for a little while. Then she became calmer, and Hildis took her a cup of ale, which she drank. She dried her tears. Gifu, a sad woman, who had grown grey in the shadows of her husband's house, comforted her as tenderly as she could; but her life had not been accustomed to tenderness. Then Edith said: 'Go away, Mother. I want Hildis.' So Hildis went to her. Edith took her by the hand and held her close and watched to see her mother go a little distance away, and then she whispered very quickly into Hildis' ear:

'Hildis, Hildis, listen, there is danger to the King. I have heard them talking, your father and mine. A heathen man named Torgils has been with them often, with others, in my father's house. They did not see me. I did not hear everything, only a little, but enough to know there will be a killing. Killing of men, Hildis. Oh Hildis, be quick and secret. Go and warn the King. Let no one see or hear you, or we shall all be killed, also.'

Hildis did not believe what she heard. She thought Edith must be very sick, perhaps bewitched, and Edith suddenly began laughing and sobbing together on the bed, and saying louder and louder to her: 'Go, Hildis, go!' Gifu ran up and took Edith in her arms and said to Hildis: 'Go, child, you cannot help her as I can.' Hildis, trembling and puzzled, wrapped her cloak about her and went out into the cold night. She heard voices over towards the hall and started to go that way. Then suddenly she stopped. She saw at a little distance across the open field a man crawling. He crawled and lay still, and then began to crawl again. She saw the long dark trail he had made crawling through the thin snow under the moon. She stood still in fear. Then she saw he was hurt. She took courage and went towards him. He raised his head, and she saw who it was. It was Duri the falconer's son. He was covered all over with snow and blood.

She ran and knelt down to him. She said: 'Duri, what has happened? Wait, I will get help.' But he put out a hand and held her skirt as she rose. 'Stay!' he whispered. He could hardly speak. 'Come close.' She bent down to him. 'Treachery,' he whispered. He lay still a while. She thought with horror that he was dead. Then he lifted his head and said, quite clearly: 'Hildis, is it you, lady?' The child Hildis answered, 'Yes, Duri, yes.' 'Hildis,' he said, 'listen carefully.' But there was a long pause. He tried several times to speak. Then at last: 'Enemy. Treachery. The valley is full of men. Hildis, the King. Warn the King. Trust no one, Hildis. Go quickly.'

He lay on his face. She bent nearer to him, and he spoke

into the ground, no longer able to raise his head: 'Go quickly, leave me. Warn the King.' But she still paused, horrified. Then she heard for the second time that night the urgent words: 'Go, go!' Weeping she turned and ran.

CHAPTER EIGHTEEN

The Pig Door

BEFORE she reached the hall she had stopped weeping. In her head she could still hear Duri's choking voice. 'Trust no one, trust no one', it said to her, over and over again. She saw people coming from the hall and stood aside while they passed. She must speak only to the King. Then she saw her brothers coming from the hall. They saw her standing there. Elric said: 'What is the matter, sister? Are you, too, crying?' For reply she only asked if the King was still at the feast.

'No, he has gone,' Elric replied. 'He went back with his company to the Dragon Hall. Elred and I would have gone with them, but our father forbade us. But Hildis, what is the matter with you? You are trembling.'

'It is Duri,' she said. 'I think he is dying. He is in the field yonder. Oh, quickly, quickly, find help!'

They looked amazed, then ran in the direction she had pointed. But she went the other way, down to the ford and over the stream, past the forge and on to the path uphill towards the trees and the Dragon Hall. A woman from the forge called to her, but she did not answer, she hurried on, running whenever she had breath enough to do so, till she reached the first trees and was in the shadows out of the moonlight. The black trees closed in around her. She stopped fearfully to listen. She heard nothing, but from where she stood she could see along the edge of the wood, where the trees were scattered among bushes and open spaces, going up the valley. For a moment she thought she had seen something glitter and move in the moonlight, some distance away up there among the bushes, between the trees. She stared; but there was nothing; all was still. Then again suddenly, a little moving cluster, which disappeared as soon as she saw it, as if it were mere fancy, a trick of the eye. With beating heart she turned and ran faster, deeper into the wood until she saw the great crossed gables of the Dragon Hall rearing up over the thorn hedge ahead of her on the far side of the clearing. For a moment she felt too weak to run farther. She sank down on one of the trees some woodmen had felled and left lying there, and sat strengthless and still for a moment, and the snow began to fall again, all round her. Getting her breath again, she stood up and ran into the clearing and across to the Dragon Hall. Little Bortric, standing guard at the gate, which was still open, saw her coming. He called to the others nearby. 'Look who is here,' he said.

She ran in and said: 'Where is the King?' The King's men came round and asked her what she wanted, and she said: 'The King, take me to the King. There is danger.'

Old Britnoth said at once: 'Close the gate!', and then to Hildis: 'What danger, little girl?'

'Men in the wood, in the valley, coming this way. Duri has been killed, he is all bleeding. Take me to the King.'

'Britnoth'! shouted one of the men from the gate, 'The gate-bars are not here! They have been taken away!'

It was a double gate, which when closed was fastened with two great bars of wood, fitted across into iron brackets. These had been there the previous night. They were there no longer. Quickly the man bound spears together to make a shaft long enough to close the gates and hold them while they found stronger timber for the purpose.

They took Hildis into the hall, where the King was. He had taken off the white tunic he had worn at the wedding, and was dressed now in plain clothes of brown and grey, such as he usually wore; but he still had the great red cloak around him. He had been reading, sitting by a taper.

'King, there is treachery,' said Britnoth. 'This girl has come to warn us. Speak up, girl.'

Hildis spoke quickly, all she knew, of what Edith had said, of Duri lying in his blood, of the men in the wood.

'And now we find the gate-bars have been taken,' said Britnoth. 'King, it is treachery, there is no doubt of it.'

The King said: 'Arm yourselves, friends. We must leave at once. Better fight in the open, if we must, than in this trap of a place. Can we get our horses from the vill? Will there be time?'

'We can try,' said Ulfstan, 'and if we fail, we may at least have time to deal with certain traitors there.'

'King Alfred,' said Guntram, 'there are two horses here already, yours and Britnoth's, which you rode back this evening from the wedding. Lord King, you yourself must go away from here, quickly. You must not be in danger. Go with Britnoth. Ride fast.'

'Guntram, I cannot leave my friends,' said the King. 'Surely we shall all have time to go together if we go now.'

Old Britnoth said: 'No, Lord King, you must take the horse, you and one other; but it will not be I. My day is over, and I am good for nothing but chopping down. But I will make tough timber. They shall see.'

They were all arming. Some went to saddle the two horses.

'What of this little girl?' said Guntram. 'She must get away at once. Run, child. We owe you much and will reward you whenever we can. But run now, you will be safe if you go at once.'

'Yes, Hildis,' said the King, 'we will not forget you. But go home now quickly.'

They led her to the gate. Some long boards had been taken down from one of the outbuildings, and men were hurriedly shaping them to fit and hold the gate, but they were not yet ready. The bound spears were still the only bar. They lifted them and opened the gate a little way for Hildis to slip through. But first Escwin looked out all round, and then drew back, and shut the gate again.

'Too late,' he said. 'Put up the bar.'

Quickly they put back the bar of spears and then peering from the wicket-shutter they looked, one after the other, and saw. Keeping near to the trees on both sides of the clearing the black shapes of men were advancing towards the Dragon Hall gate. Axe and sword and shield and spear they saw. They saw the grey shine of moonlight on moving helmets. They saw warfare and the heathen.

'Very well', said one. 'It comes at last. I have expected this all my life.'

'Very well', said the King, when they told him. 'My friends, I am sorry to have led you by mischance into this bad place. If there is still anything I can do to save you I will do it. If not, I will die with you, and be in good company. Let us pray to God, for there is now no way out.'

Then, breaking into the hard mood of men ready for battle, came the words of the child Hildis. She stood, hardly more than belt high between two great men in iron. She spoke urgently:

'King Alfred,' she cried, 'there is a way out. The Pig Door!'

This was the name the children had given to that hole in the hedge, hidden low down, which the pigs had made years ago. The children still used it now and again, and only the children knew of it. It had grown a little narrower with the years, but it was still open. 'Come and see,' she cried.

From the other side of the gate a heathen voice suddenly shouted:

'King Alfred! Open the gate and come out! We will spare your life. Come out!'

The new bar that had been fashioned for the gate was still not properly finished, but it was the best that could now be done. They fixed it somehow across the brackets and judged it would hold for a while. The heathen shouted again from the clearing outside: 'Open and come out!' Hildis meanwhile had tugged at Ulfstan's sleeve and led him, running, to the hole in the hedge behind the shed. He ran back in a hurry to the others and said:

'It will do! It is very narrow, but the King and as many others as possible could get through and away, while the rest of us keep the enemy here at the gate. Who goes with the King? Quickly!'

'All must go or I cannot', said the King. 'I will not crawl through a hole to live, while my friends die here to save me.'

Then said Guntram:

'My Lord King Alfred, you are not free to choose. We few are likely to die here in any case; it will be a pity, but it will make no great difference. But you, if you die here like this, the whole realm of Wessex will die with you, and the whole of Christendom in this quarter of the world will fall. If it were some great battle, with all your folk in arms around you, that would be a different thing. There, if you died, it would be seen and known by all for a proper death, and no fault of yours. But if you die here, like this, none will know of it. It will be as if you had secretly stolen away and abandoned your people. You yourself have set the standards by which this kingdom now is ruled. But your work is only at its beginning. You cannot be spared from it. All still depends upon you. Therefore you must go back to your kingdom, King Alfred. We will look after this piece of it for as long as we can.'

The thanes and warriors of the King acclaimed this speech, every one of them. The King stood with a white face, and looked from each to each. Each face answered him in the same way. He knew well that what they said was true. He bowed his head and said: 'Very well, I will go. As many as possible come with me.'

From beyond the hedge the heathen shouted:

'Come out, Saxon pigs, come out of your stye! Come out of the gate, King Alfred! We shall fetch you out roughly if we have to come in!'

'Let them come in if they can,' said old Britnoth. 'I wait for them. By the Almighty, I have something left for them, even now. Where is my son Wulfhere, whom they slew?

Farewell, King Alfred, get you gone now. Never fear for me.'

Hildis led the way to the Pig Door. Bortric and Escwin had been chosen to go first with the King. Others came behind. Hildis crouched and wriggled through the hole, to show the crooked way it went. She feared it would be very narrow for the others. The thorns tore her clothes as she crawled through. On the far side there was no enemy to be seen and the trees were close at hand. It was beginning to snow hard, and one could not see far away. Little Bortric scrambled through. He had had to leave his shield behind, but he brought his axe. He was badly cut by the thorns in the narrow way. Then came the King. His great red cloak he had thrown aside. It would be too conspicuous and in any case was too big for the narrow hole. As he came through, his head, hands and his clothes were all cut and torn. He came out with great difficulty, bleeding and ragged. Bortric dragged him out and pulled him into the cover of the trees, with Hildis. Escwin followed soon after. Then Bortric whispered: 'Listen!' He signalled quickly to go further into the wood. He had heard men coming around the corner of the great hedge farther along. The enemy were coming to see what way they could find to break in. 'Run!' said Bortric. Escwin and Hildis and the King ran farther into the wood, which went uphill. Bortric came behind, stopping to look back. He saw the next of the King's men, whose name was Helm, crawl out of the hole and stand up, but only just in time to meet the heathen as they came along the hedge. They ran shouting towards him, and he started running for the wood. Bortric saw then that the heathen following him might come searching into the wood. To prevent it he ran down the hill to the place where Helm was standing to face the enemy. Swinging his axe Bortric ran forward. The enemy gave ground and went no farther into the wood but all turned upon Helm and Bortric, who stood now with their backs against the hedge. This was the end for them both, but it took a long time and the King all the while was climbing higher and farther into the wood.

The hillside grew steeper. The King paused for breath. Escwin, holding Hildis by the hand, came up with him.

'Where is Bortric, where are the others?' asked the King. 'Do you hear fighting back there?'

'They will be coming after us, lord,' said Escwin. 'We must keep moving. They will follow our tracks.'

They pressed on upwards to the top of the ridge, where the wood opened and showed a steep descent the other side into a valley. They hurried down into it. In the open it was snowing hard. They found sheltering trees again farther on and stopped to listen. A great silence lay on everything, silent as the falling snow. Nobody followed them. They were alone.

'Lord,' said Escwin, 'we can do nothing now but go on.'

'God give them strength,' said the King. He covered his scratched face with his scratched and bloody hands. 'God, forgive me, where are they, what have I led them into?'

The silent wood held them all in stillness for a while. Then the King dropped his hands and lifted his head and said:

'So be it then. We must make our way south, to Shaftesbury or Sherborne, whichever we can. But what can we do for this child, Escwin? Look, she is spent.'

Hildis, leaning against Escwin and shivering now with cold and fatigue, was swaying on her feet.

'We must carry her,' said the King. 'Help her on to my back first, and put my cloak over her.' It was a brown cloak which Ulfstan had given him when he threw away his other. Escwin put it around Hildis on the King's back, and thus they set off again. Hildis slept.

CHAPTER NINETEEN

The End of the Dragon Hall

BRITNOTH was told that Helm and Bortric had been killed fighting at the Pig Door, and that no one else could now escape that way. But would the heathen attempt to come in there?

'The first one that does,' said Britnoth, 'let him but put his head through, and he will lie there and block the passage for ever. But is the King safe?'

This was answered by the heathen themselves, shouting once again outside: 'Come out, King Alfred! We will give you your life if you come out now.'

Britnoth grinned. 'They do not know,' he said. 'All is well. So now we go to work, to keep ourselves warm.'

The hedge of thorns was so dense and high that nothing could be seen through it; but they set a ladder against the roof of the hall, and Ulfstan went up to report what he could see. A flight of arrows bit into the roof around him and drove him down. Although the falling snow had made it difficult to see well, he reckoned that there were a hundred heathen in view, and doubtless there were more among the trees. The Saxons behind the gate numbered three and twenty.

Eclac, son of Wulfric, was at the loophole of the gate. He said: 'They are coming!' A moment later there came a shower of blows upon the gate, as a heavy mob of the heathen thrust against it to burst it open. The Saxons stood shield to shield in a rank, waiting for the gate to give; but the improvised bars held firm, and after many attempts the heathen withdrew from this assault. Then said Britnoth:

'We have two horses, ready saddled. It might be possible for two of us to get away, to warn Ethelnoth and the others.

Maybe they might find help for us. We could choose a moment like this to open the gate. It is worth trying. Why waste the horses?'

This was agreed. It was also agreed that Guntram should be one of those to go. He protested, but it was agreed by all that he was most suitable. Chosen with him for this venture was Oslac, a thane's son and a good horseman. They said farewell to their friends there at the Dragon Hall. They armed themselves and mounted into their saddles. Guntram looked like a giant in his great helmet and Frankish mail. But then once more Ulfstan climbed the ladder, and in the snowy night he saw the heathen advancing again to the gate. They came in a great mass, carrying the trunk of a pine tree, one of those which the woodmen had felled and left lying.

'They will break the gate this time', said Ulfstan. 'What can you do now, Guntram?'

Guntram said: 'We will go at once, while they are all cumbered with the tree. Open and close the gate quickly. But wait till they are very near, for then they will least expect it.'

Ulfstan watched through the loophole till the heathen were nearly at the gate with the tree. They were all together holding the tree, and on each side of the gate were others ready armed to rush in when the gate broke, but unprepared for any other move. Then at a signal the Saxons opened the gates and Oslac and Guntram suddenly rode out galloping, shouting their war-cries and striking with their swords as they went. They rode straight down the line of the tree, one on each side. In confusion the tree carriers dropped their burden and ran away. Meanwhile at once the Saxons closed the gate again, and barred it up. Three or four of the heathen who had too boldly rushed in ahead of the rest were quickly killed.

Guntram and Oslac galloped across the clearing, but at the far side a great crowd of the pagans came out of the trees on foot towards them. The two turned to ride away in another direction, but Oslac here was unlucky. His horse slipped in the snow, and though he did not fall, in stopping and steadying he lost enough time for the nearest pagans to catch and surround him. He laid about him with his sword and fought like a boar at bay, but he could not break the ring that hemmed him in, and he was killed there after a hard fight. But Guntram, not stopping, galloped around the clearing the other way. The snow had stopped falling and in the light reflected from the white ground he could see his way well. He also saw two men on horseback in the clearing, one of whom he judged to be the leader of the attackers. Him he did not know, but the other he saw clearly and knew at once. He reined in his horse, even there with the heathen after him, and turned about once more. Then at a gallop he rode straight towards the man on horseback.

'Unferth!' he shouted, swinging his great sword. 'Die, traitor!'

Unferth wheeled his horse, but not in time. Guntram's sword came down on him with all its force. Unferth cried out. As he fell, Guntram struck him again, then turned and rode full pelt at the thicket mob of the enemy, shouting as he went. They opened out and ran from in front of him, ran from the galloping horse, the swinging sword. He went through into the woodland and down the path and away. None caught him. He went down to the river bank and along the road to Bruton, alone and clear.

It was Jarl Torgils Auk who commanded the heathen. Surprised, like Unferth, at Guntram's sudden charge he had been unable himself to do more than wheel aside. He saw Unferth fall and lie bleeding on the ground, and dismounted to help him. But Unferth was dead, his skull cloven in two. 'That was a quick death,' said Torgils, 'and too soon for my liking. Who is there now to point out the King for me? I shall not know which is which.' Guthorm had bidden him to take King Alfred alive if he could; but alive or dead he was to find him and bring him to Guthorm. 'There is no help for it now,

but to kill them all' said Torgils to Olaf Skald, who was with him on that night's work.

So the heathen returned to the gate, and picked up the tree, and ran with it all together against the gate, which shook and cracked at the first blow. At the second blow it cracked and rocked on the gateposts; and at the third it burst and fell in. The heathen swarmed over the fallen gate and into the yard.

The Saxons met them shield to shield. They drove them back twice over the fallen gate, and covered the timbers of it with dead men. But they themselves lost seven of their comrades in the fighting and the fourteen who were left were not now enough to hold the gateway any longer, for they had been fighting for an hour. So Britnoth cried: 'Back now into the hall. There we can take turns to hold the narrow door.' So they backed away towards the Dragon Hall, and the heathen spread into the yard. One of them then saw the great red cloak King Alfred had cast off, still lying in the yard where he had left it. He went and picked it up. But Ulfstan saw him, and ran at him shouting: 'Thief! Dog!' and struck him down. He picked up the cloak and slung it on his shoulder, and ran back towards the hall door where his friends stood like a wall, with their swords ready. But Torgils had seen the cloak. It had been well described to him by Unferth as a garment the King was wearing. He remembered it. He called to his men to seize the cloak and they all ran against Ulfstan before he could reach the door, and Ulfstan laughed grimly. He stood and faced them all. 'You want the King's cloak, Northmen?' he mocked them. 'Then come this way and get it!' He ran again towards the door and four came out to him, and there they fought around the King's cloak. It had come a long way from the sunny weaving-room in Tuscany, from the soft hands of the embroidresses singing together at their work, from the parade and the sound of trumpets when the Emperor Charles had first put it on and the Pope of Rome had blessed him in it, to this place where five men died in the snow trying to keep it from an enemy. The enemy took it in the end.

Britnoth and Eclac and seven others were left in the Dragon Hall, behind the barred door. They drank and refreshed themselves. They said they would sell their lives dear when the time came, but now they could wait and rest a little.

Outside, Jarl Torgils said: 'We have not all night to spend here. Let us smoke them out, and make an end of it.'

But even this took time. The heathen had come secretly in the dark, without torches. They sent men back to the vill to bring fire, but when it came they had further difficulty. Britnoth inside the hall said grimly: 'I guess what they are doing. They are trying to set fire to the roof. But the thatch is too wet with all this snow. We can rest a little longer yet, before we go out.'

Britnoth's guess was good as far as it went, but his rest did not last long. The wet thatch was hard to kindle, but, once it was well alight, it and the old dry wood of the roof blazed up like tinder. Those within the hall saw the red mouth of fire opening over their heads. They took up their shields again and prepared to go out. But still they kept Torgils waiting.

The fire spread rapidly along the roof. The golden dragon of the gable coiled glittering in the red night. The snow all round the Dragon Hall melted and steamed in the heat. The heathen waited. Then at last the doors opened and the nine came out. Bright light now, like a hundred torches, shone down upon the fighting. Jarl Torgils regretted his many men that lay dead before the Saxons were finished. It was near morning. The Dragon Hall was blazing upwards into the sky like the funeral pyre of a king. 'As is fitting,' said Olaf Skald, 'for so indeed it is.' 'Indeed it is, it must be so,' replied Torgils. 'None have escaped except that one man, he who killed Unferth.' The thought passed through his mind that this man might after all have been the King; but he put the thought from him. Alfred had been described as a slightly built man, and this man had been too big.

Now at the blazing Dragon Hall a part of the roof fell inwards, and the fire leaped out of the hole it made, still higher into the black sky, carrying upwards a cloud of whirling sparks. The heathen had all drawn back out of the heat in the yard. The great thorn hedge itself was singeing and smoking, ready to burn. The Saxons all lay within, now to the last man dead or dying. But one final scene remained. From over the fallen gateway, with the glaring fire behind him, starkly standing, not yet dead though covered with wounds, old Britnoth came, his sword still in his hand. He walked forward with painful steps, bending, supporting himself on the sword, till he stood within the wide half-circle of the silent heathen. Not one of them moved. Britnoth halted. He stood himself upright with great difficulty. His shield arm, though shieldless, he lifted now firmly before him. His sword in his right hand he raised, but very slowly, till he had it high over his head, the point upwards. And then, there and thus died old Britnoth, and pitched forward like a tree, his whole upright length, fallen upon his face.

In the wide circle of the heathen Danes there began a tapping noise. It spread around the circle, growing louder and louder above the rushing and spitting noises of the fire, till it was like a great battering of iron drums. The heathen were beating with their weapons upon their shields. This was their salute to Britnoth, at his life's end.

CHAPTER TWENTY

The Old Enemy

STILLNESS in the snow-whitened woods. Slowness of a last few snowflakes floating down the silent sky. Silence of white pathways lost among unmoving trees. Frost and silence.

The two men with the little girl asleep moved forward step after step. They came presently to a stream. It was shallow, and they crossed it without pausing to take off their shoes, their feet and legs wet through already from the snow. On the bank Escwin said: 'It is now my turn to carry the child.' The King did not protest at this. He had been walking more slowly than at first and with increasing difficulty. He said:

'I fear after all I may not be able to go any great distance tonight.'

Escwin said: 'My lord, are you sick?'

'It is my old enemy,' said the King. 'It comes at an unlucky time. However, I must keep moving so long as I can. At least I must go on till we can find some sort of shelter. This enemy is not yet here in strength. Lead on, Escwin.'

Escwin lifted Hildis from the King's back. She awoke now, and asked where she was. She said she was cold. They thought it would warm her to walk a little, and so she did, but after a while Escwin lifted her onto his back and carried her again, because of her frequent stumbling. He told her they were going southwards, towards Shaftesbury. It would be a long way. She asked when would she go home again. 'Later,' said Escwin.

The trees opened out, and they could see the steep slope which formed the western ramparts of the great Wessex Down, lying on their left. They went on step by step, putting their feet step after step into the uncertain depths of snow. They came nearer the high hillside. The King paused from time to time. He steadied himself against the trees.

'Now as soon as we find shelter,' he said presently, 'I shall have to lie there and hide. Another mile or two is likely to be the most I can do. You must make sure of the place, Escwin, and go on alone. Bring help as soon as you can. It is the only way.'

'I will do it,' said Escwin. 'But what about the child here?'

Hildis, who was now awake, said: 'I will stay with my lord the King, and help him.'

'There will be little you can do, Hildis,' said the King. 'But one thing is certain: you must not call me King. I shall be in hiding to save my life. Do you understand that?'

She said she understood.

'You are a good child,' said the King, 'and I shall be glad of your company. But I am likely to seem very sick for a little while, and you must not be alarmed by it. It will pass. Now let us move on.'

They went on again, step after step. They went uphill and down, and found no shelter. The rampart of the Great Down now lay directly upon their left. The King faltered in his step and sank down, holding his head. But he pulled himself up onto his feet again. 'Keep on,' he said. They kept on a little farther. A wind had started to blow, the moon darkened. Escwin feared more snow was coming. But then, stirred by the wind, they heard, not far ahead of them a sound like a cowbell clanking. Escwin said: 'Wait here,' and while the King rested he went forward quickly, following the noise. He came back in a short while.

'There is a little chapel,' he said. 'It is all in ruins, but it is shelter.'

He and Hildis helped the King to his feet again and they went to the chapel. The little bell was clanking from a branch overhead. The place must have been the cell of some hermit years ago, but now it was deserted, and filled to the roof with new straw.

'Thank God,' said the King. 'It has been His mercy to save us.'

Hildis and Escwin were shivering, but the King was sweating with the heat of his sickness. They crept into the ruined chapel and hollowed out a place in the straw. They pulled it right over them, huddling all together to keep warm. Hildis slept; the King shivered and sweated; and Escwin waited for the daylight. The new snow blotted out all their footprints in the forest outside.

CHAPTER TWENTY-ONE

The Panic of Wessex

KING GUTHORM with three thousand men had stormed across the border land into Wessex, suddenly and ferociously. Neither house nor farm, village or town had any warning. With greatest secrecy he had left his camp at Gloucester, before even a hint of his preparation had been rumoured abroad. Surprise was complete. The pagans came down the Roman road from Cirencester in the night and broke into Chippenham town while the gate-watch was asleep, all unwarned, and there they slaughtered every person regardless of age or sex who offered the least resistance to them. They hanged the town-reeve and the priest, one in each town gateway, at the two ends of the street. They plundered every house and set fire to many. Guthorm with his jarls Einar and Asbiorn rode grimly on horseback through the midst of it all. Great satisfaction swelled in Guthorm's breast.

'King Alfred said he would teach me a lesson if I ever came to Wessex again,' said he. 'Now is his chance to do it. I have sent for him.'

He had sent Torgils Auk with two hundred picked men, all on good horses.

'Bring me back King Alfred, dead or alive, himself or his head,' were Guthorm's instructions. 'But alive if possible. It will please me to do some teaching myself.'

Torgils and the raiding party had crossed the border very secretly the night before Guthorm and the main army. They had lain hidden all next day in the depths of Selwood. Unferth's messenger had led them to a prepared spot. They had a hope to catch King Alfred in the forest as he was hunting; but this came to nothing. When dusk fell they moved from their hiding-place and came to Alham. At that time Guthorm was riding towards Chippenham, and the panic of Wessex had begun.

Fifteen miles east of Chippenham, at a place called Woodborough, lay the vill of Ethelhelm, ealdorman of Wiltshire. Here that night young Ethelhelm lay asleep, unsuspecting. But as Guthorm was entering Chippenham, Jarl Sigurd Hammerfist, with five hundred men descended upon Woodborough vill. A churl of Ethelhelm's had seen them at a distance and had just time to come running from the fields to raise the alarm; but there was no time to organize a defence. There was only time enough for Ethelhelm to send away his wife and child with some of his house-thanes to guard them and for him and the rest of his household to arm themselves, before the heathen storm was upon them. They fought and were slain there that night, young Ethelhelm and all the rest, and Jarl Sigurd sacked the vill, and Wiltshire had no ealdorman next day, and the men of Wiltshire did not know where to turn. The shire-reeve at Amesbury rallied as many as he could, but they were not yet ready when the heathen flood came upon them also, down the valley from captured Woodborough, and so they fled, and Amesbury was taken. This New Year was the worst time Wessex ever knew.

Farther to the east the men of Berkshire also awoke that morning to find the heathen once more at their thresholds. King Osketil in his lands of Mercia, though not himself prepared to lead the new invasion of Wessex, was ready to take advantage of it. There were still many unsatisfied adventurers in eastern Mercia, and more still likely to come in, the moment success against Wessex could at last be assured. So in the next few days a force of the Danes sacked Abingdon and Dorchester, and threatened the whole wide valley of the Thames. The people of Reading packed up their goods and fled south over the snow, leaving the town half-empty, as they had once done before, seven years earlier. Ealdorman Sigeric armed himself and sent out the war-trumpet, but the men who gathered now into their scattered levies were bewildered by rumours and bad news of every kind which no one seemed able to refute. Sigeric sent messengers to the King at Winchester, but they returned saying the King was not there, and there were fears for his safety.

In Chippenham Guthorm eagerly awaited Torgils' return. All day he had kept men on the look-out, to bring him word the very moment the returning raiding-party was seen. The raiders did not in fact reach Chippenham town until after dark. They were weary with fighting and riding. Guthorm met them at the town gate. Jarl Torgils dismounted wearily and walked with cramped legs.

'Welcome, Torgils,' said Guthorm. 'Have you King Alfred with you? Is he alive or dead?'

'He is dead,' said Torgils. 'Be easy. But he is not here. Instead I have brought your new king of Wessex. There he is yonder.'

Edgar, Ethelbalt's son, sat among the horsemen looking more like a captive than a king. Guthorm gave him not so much as a glance.

'Not here?' he bellowed at Torgils. 'Not his body? Not even his head? What have you brought then? How are you sure he is dead? Could you not take him alive? What happened?'

Torgils said: 'We did everything possible, King Guthorm. We would have caught Alfred alive in the forest, but Unferth's plan miscarried. In the end we had to surround the King and his men all together in the hall where they lodged. The King would not give himself up. They fought like wild boars at bay to the very end, every one of them. I tell you we had a hard time of it, King Guthorm; but we did the work for you just as you wanted.'

'How, as I wanted! What proof have you?' demanded Guthorm angrily. 'Why did you not bring his head?'

'We did not know which he was. Would you have us bring

them all? Unferth, who came to point him out to us, was killed.'

'Ha!' Guthorm exclaimed. 'So that settles my debt with him. How did that happen?'

Torgils told him simply that it happened in the fighting. But he said nothing about the horseman who had ridden away after the slaying of Unferth.

Guthorm pressed him to say how he was certain the King had been there in the beleagured hall, and Torgils said Unferth had seen him go in, had recognized him clearly, face, clothes and all.

'And here is a trophy I bring you,' he concluded. 'It is the cloak King Alfred was wearing. See all the blood upon it.'

Guthorm took the cloak and handled it, turning it this way and that.

'You are sure it is his?'

'Whose else could it be? Look at it, none other had anything like it.'

'None other had a head like his, either,' said Guthorm. 'I would rather have had that. However, this is better than nothing. Come to my house, then, and drink, and tell me more.'

Sitting with the ale-horn between them Guthorm questioned Torgils again and again about every detail of the fight.

'So the whole place was burned to the ground, and the King's body and the rest along with it, you say. And none escaped, not one?'

'By the gods!' exclaimed Torgils at last, rising to his feet. 'How many times must I tell you? It was impossible.'

'Very well, very well', said Guthorm. 'Very well, then, it will do.'

This was as much thanks as Torgils got for his trouble. Guthorm went out and fetched Edgar from his guards. He brought him by the arm into the house and held a torch close to his face, to see him better.

'Well, then, if you're to be king of Wessex you'd better get to know me,' he said. 'You will need to. Here, drink and eat.'

Asbiorn came in late with the news of the death of Ethelhelm at Woodborough. Guthorm suddenly began to be in better spirits.

'It is going well', he said. 'Now spread the news everywhere, Alfred, King of Wessex, is dead! Shout it out in every village. Let the Saxons grind their teeth upon that!'

He was right in his belief of what this news would do. After all their years of constant watchfulness and fighting, suddenly to be taken by surprise like this in midwinter, finding themselves once again in the teeth of the wretched war against the everlasting enemy, finding themselves without any army in the field, with great nobles known to be slain at their hearths and the King himself reported dead, the people of Wessex lost heart. They left their houses and fled, as people everywhere had fled in East Anglia, in Mercia, in Northumbria and all over Europe, at the dreaded approach of the furious and unconquerable Northmen. What use in fighting further?

On a table in Guthorm's house, with the smell of roasting meat-fat and the stable-stink of tethered horses for incense, the three wooden gods, Odin, Thor and Frey stood in a row. Guthorm brought King Alfred's cloak and laid it out on the table in front of them.

'There's that, so far', he said. 'It'll do to wrap you up in, next time we travel. You deserve the best. You are doing well for us all. Guthorm gives you thanks.'

The three gods, unmoving, grinned at him as usual.

CHAPTER TWENTY-TWO

Bread

ESCWIN saw the daylight at last, through the chinks of the wall. He pushed aside the straw that covered him, and went and looked out at the door. It was no longer snowing. Then he drew back quickly. He had seen a man coming through the trees towards the chapel-hut. Escwin watched through the chinks. The man was a peasant, a poor woodlander, whose age might be judged only by his thickness and toughness, like a tree. He plodded through the snow towards the chapel, but before he reached the door Escwin stepped out and confronted him. The man at once turned in fright, as if to run away, but Escwin said quickly:

'I am a friend. There are three of us here, sheltering from the weather. We shall go soon. You can help us.'

The man said: 'Go now. I cannot help people. Are you outlaws?'

Escwin explained they were two travellers and a child benighted in the snow, and that one was sick and unable to move. It was needful to fetch help. He asked how far they were from Shaftesbury.

'That is ten mile or more, so they say,' said the man. 'I myself did never go there. Two mile yonder, up the hill, there is my master's village, Penselwood.'

Escwin asked who his master was. The man said:

'He is Cutha the Churl, a friend of Witred the thane. Witred's lord is the ealdorman himself, so I have heard.'

Escwin asked which ealdorman?

'That I could not say,' replied the man. 'No ealdorman comes here. But Witred I have seen. Now, master, I have come to fetch clean straw for the oxen and for my wife who is in childbed. I must go in and get it.'

He pushed past Escwin into the chapel, where the King and Hildis were awake. The King had tried to stand, but could not. He lay back pale and shivering. The man took no notice, but pulled away at the straw till he had a great bundle, which he tied with a rope. Escwin asked if he wanted help.

'Why, you could bring a load and save me coming again,' said the man. So Escwin bundled a load and tied it with his belt, and slung it onto his back, and followed the man along the path into the trees. As they went the man said:

'That one in there, he has the sweats. He should lie by the hearth, not out there in the cold. I will speak to the old woman.'

When Escwin returned to the chapel half an hour later he found the King sitting up. Hildis had packed him round with straw. She was herself shivering.

'The peasant's cottage lies about half a mile off,' he said. 'There is a fire and a family and a pig and a couple of oxen. It is warm. Can you walk there, lord?'

'I fear not yet,' said the King. 'But this child should go. And you, Escwin, must go at once to Alfgar at Shaftesbury. I will wait for you here. With luck you might get help and be back again before dark. I will have recovered by then, enough to sit on a horse. But now at this moment I cannot stand.'

So Escwin took his sword from under the straw where he had hidden it, and slung it over his shoulder, and wrapped his cloak tightly about him, and set off briskly, going south.

'Hildis,' said the King, 'you too must go now and find the cottage, and keep warm,' But she would not go at first. She went about keeping warm by collecting sticks, with which she made a heap in the clearing not far outside the door. Then she went away in the direction of the cottage, and did not come back for some time. When she did come she was carrying a little clay pot full of glowing charcoal. It was wrapped round with a rag so that she could carry it, and she had to stop and blow on it every now and again, to keep it alive. With this and some straw and great patience she kindled a fire, and in the pot she melted snow-water and warmed it, and took it to the King. He had been sleeping. When he awoke he was shivering, but this time only from the cold, not from the fever. He drank the warm water gladly, and came out and warmed himself by the crackling fire. The ground all round it was wet with the snow it had melted, but in the mud he and the girl crouched and warmed themselves.

The day wore on, and Escwin did not return. The fire died down and Hildis could find no more fuel to hand, though she roamed farther away into the wood for it. It presently began to grow very cold again, and more snow began to fall. The King said at last:

'We must go to the cottage, for I see we shall have to spend another night in the forest, and we have not enough heat left in us to warm the straw. So lead the way, Hildis. My sickness is beginning to pass. Tomorrow I shall be well enough to go any distance.'

He followed Hildis, going as fast as he could in spite of the pain and dizziness he still had. They went for about half a mile with the steep hillside on their left, and presently turned a corner of the hill into a wooded combe. There stood the cottage. It was a long, low, rough place, partly dug down into the ground, so that it was like a long shallow pit with a shaggy roof pitched over it; and the roof being covered now with snow it might all have passed notice as a rocky hump of earth but for the trodden ground and litter all about it and the dirty smoke-hole in the mounded roof. The door-hole was covered with a curtain of ox-hide, which moved as Hildis and the King approached, and an old woman came out of it and watched them, her wrinkled, shaky fingers busy all the time with her distaff and spindle. The old woman was clothed in thick shabby garments of blackish-green; but the King, with scratched face and torn clothing, with muddy legs and uncombed hair, and with his pale face, looked even more wretched and poor than she.

It was snowing thickly again. Without a word she let them into the cottage.

Inside, the light was dim. The floor was all composed of earth mixed with refuse trodden down hard. From the roof-beams hung all the family's gear, hanks of cloth and wool, dried herbs, rope-ends, beans, bundles of wooden stakes, and wooden tools. Over the hearth-fire was suspended the family's one object of value, the great iron pot. Hot water was simmering in it. In the dirt by the fire a little boy about three years old was lying fast asleep. Beyond, in a corner, lay the peasant's wife, nursing a new-born baby. Beyond her again, fenced off with a rail and a number of old boards were the two oxen and the pig which Escwin had spoken of. The whole place was warm and stinking. The King could hardly bring himself to enter it, with his sick stomach and his reeling head; but he could not go back into the snow. He sat himself down against the wall.

Hildis had brought the little clay pot with her, and she gave it back now to the old woman, who said: 'What ails him?' jerking her head towards the pale King. Hildis said: 'A passing thing, mother. He will be well soon.' The old woman said: 'Can he work? The man is away to the village and the baby born just an hour ago, it is more than I can manage at my age.' Hildis said: 'I can help you, mother.' She fetched in kale from the stack outside, to feed the cattle, and she helped wash the new baby. 'Another boy, poor thing', said the old woman. 'You will want food,' she said. In what was left of the hot water she began to make porridge, carefully measuring out the meal by palmfuls from a crock. 'Only a little left,' she said; 'it has been a bad year.'

It was growing dark again. The man came in, back from the village, and kicked the snow off his feet.

'Has that come yet, the poor thing?' he asked.

'Another boy,' said the old woman.

'Ah,' said the man. He went and looked a while at the baby, then sat down with his porridge beside the wife. The King with closed eyes heard them talking from time to time. It was dark outside, firelight the only light within. The beasts at the far end shifted and grunted in the straw. The old woman busy again with her distaff and spindle was sitting singing half to herself, half to the baby in the straw. Hildis, nodding half-asleep, for she had slept little all that frozen night before, was playing with the three-year-old boy, to keep him from crying for more porridge.

The King was thinking: What has happened to Escwin? What is happening in all my kingdom now, while I am lost here in this dark hole? He got himself to his feet and went to the door to peer out. Outside, it was blowing thick and fast with snow. The man's voice said across the dark hole of the cottage:

'That friend of yours will not find his way back in this, master. Best to hope he doesn't try, poor thing.'

The King returned to his place by the wall. He knew that whatever kingdom he once had was now reduced, for this night at least and perhaps for ever, to no more than a cottage hearth, a peasant with his wife and baby, an old woman, two children, and some stinking animals. The warm bodies of these were all that lay between him and the cold wind. They now all began to wrap themselves down in the straw, to go to sleep; and so in the end did he.

When he awoke it was daylight once again. There was a noise going on, the grinding round and round of a quern. The old woman was sitting by the hearth grinding corn. Handful by handful she carefully put in the grain, round and round she ground the quern. The man had gone out again, back to his daily labour somewhere away in the snowy forest. The baby was crying. The mother was no longer in bed but was kneading dough on a plank by the fire, opposite the old woman with the quern. When she had finished kneading she took a broom of twigs and swept a clean place on the hot hearthstones. But then she stood up and bent over, holding her hands to her back, moaning a little. The old woman said:

'Go and lie down again, daughter. I will do all this.'

She led the mother back to the straw, and gave her the baby to nurse. The little boy came running to her saying he was hungry. The old woman saw that Hildis was still asleep and went over and shook her. 'Give me a hand, girl,' she said. Hildis sleepily got up and looked around her in a sudden fright at the unfamiliar place. The King then stood up and said: 'She is still half-asleep, mother. Let me help.'

'Why, then, fetch in wood for the fire, and fodder for the cattle,' the old woman said. 'There's more than enough to do here.'

The King went out. His illness had gone again at last. The snow was shining in the early morning sun under a bright sky. 'Escwin will be here soon, with the others,' said the King to himself. But then, what others? Where were Britnoth and the rest? What had happened at Alham? What were the heathen doing in Wessex? What should the King do now? Should he wait here for Escwin, or go on alone? Then he thought: 'I should be carrying in logs and cattle-feed.' He found the wood-pile and took care to pull out the dryest wood, which he carried in. The old woman had finished grinding the corn, and she was tying the little supply of flour into a cloth bag.

'Look,' she said, 'that is the last of it, unless the man can get more from Churl Cutha. A bad harvest it was. The man may have to sell his freedom. We cannot eat freedom, master.'

She hung the bag of flour on a peg from the roof-beam. She sent off Hildis, who had been kneading the dough, to take care of the little boy, who was running about crying. She sprinkled flour on the hearthstone and started to make up the dough into little cakes, which she set to bake at the fire. The King went out to the kale-stack and brought in fodder for the cattle.

'Acorns and bran for the sow, in the bin over there,' said the old woman. 'We must keep her alive somehow, poor thing, or we shall have no piglets this year.'

The King fed the thin sow her watery mash of bran and acorns. The old woman's daughter was moaning in bed with pains in her back and the old woman went over to rub her. She said to the King as she went:

'Master, watch the bread-cakes, turn them, or they will burn.'

The King turned the bread-cakes on the hearth. Hildis, who was holding the baby to quieten it, came over to him.

'Lord,' she said, 'will Thane Escwin come soon? What can have happened to my brothers and my mother?'

The King could not answer her. He would willingly have soothed her fears, but he could not forget the treachery that had taken place at Alham. He did not know how deep it went, nor how wide it spread. It was possible that the whole region of Alham and Sherborne, perhaps the whole shire of Somerset, was in the hands of the heathen. For all he knew, Escwin might never have found help; he might be lying dead in the snow, only a mile or two away. 'I cannot stay here like this, waiting,' the King said to himself, 'I must act.' He rose to his feet, and went to the door again. Should he set off now, at once, and make his own way to Shaftesbury? The sun was well up in the sky. He would wait for Escwin only a little longer, then go he must, alone. The little girl would come to no harm here with the peasants. He would send for her later.

He went and sat down again to wait a few more minutes. He was deep in thought. Hildis said something to him, but he hardly heard her, and she went away, taking the crying baby back to its mother. The King, his head in his hands, prayed for strength and hope. If the enemy had once again attacked in full force, they had caught him this time utterly unprepared. What now could he do to mend matters? It would take seven or eight weeks at least, to concentrate a force large enough for a pitched battle. Communications were bad at this time of year. The problem would be how to keep the fighting spirit of West Saxons alive in their hearts until Easter-tide; then he could lead them fresh into the field, when the enemy's first driving power was exhausted. He could do that. He had done it before.

'Yes, he had done it before, and now it was all to be done again. In his mind's eye he saw again the awful and familiar scenes, the plundered town, the warrior dead in the beaten-down cornfield, the woman dead in the farmyard, the burning homestead. The sour reek of burning, he could smell it in his nostrils, even now.

A loud and anguished cry brought his mind back to the cottage hearth. He sat upright, and as he did so he felt a violent blow on the shoulder. It was the old woman. She had struck him. She struck him again. He sprang to his feet in anger, but then saw that the old woman was now down upon her knees at the hearth, pulling away the cakes of bread as fast as she could They were all black and burning, very little left of them but smoking crust and cinder.

'Look, look, look!' the old woman was shouting. 'Could you smell nothing; could you see nothing?' She put her head in her hands and rocked herself back and forth on the hearth, bowed low, as the King had been only a minute before. The King pulled the rest of the burning cakes away from the fire. He could find nothing to say. The old woman went on:

'What were you thinking of? See, this is our food, our bread. It is all very well for the man and me, we can eat it like this, we can soak it in water and eat it, we shall have to do so, for it is all the food we have. But there is that little one, and there is that daughter of mine over there, who is sick; must they eat cinders, too, because you are a fool with no eyes? You'd have been ready enough to eat it, I'm sure. Could you not have watched it?'

'Old mother, I am sorry,' was all the King could find to say.

The old woman rose to her feet and went and fetched a crock of water and started soaking the burnt cakes in it, all the time talking almost as if to herself:

'Working and starving, working and starving. What else is there? Working and eating sometimes. If it is not a bad harvest year, then it will be a war year. Seven years ago my man and my son went away. They went with his lordship the thane, to fight in the wars with him, somewhere away in Hampshire, far away. They never came back, not even the lord thane. What good did it do? Working and starving and burnt bread is all we get in the end. It isn't worth fighting for. But then, on top of all that, to be stupid and careless! Where do you come from, master? I can see you're not one of our sort. Bread is precious stuff to us. Hard work it is to get it.'

Before the King could find an answer there came the noise of someone running. It was the man. He came in at the door, panting for breath.

'Quick,' he gasped out. 'Come away, mother, quickly, bring the children; wife, get up, come away and hide! Armed men, soldiers are coming!'

'Who are they?' asked the King, jumping to his feet. 'What banner do they carry?'

'What is that, a banner?' the man replied. 'They have weapons, that is all I know. They are strangers. They are all at that place where I keep the straw. Is it for you, master?'

Hildis and the King ran out of the cottage, just as, round the flank of the hill, Escwin the King's thane on a black horse came galloping, scattering the snow. Close behind him, with a great company, with all clinking and flashing of hauberk and helmet, of sword-pommel, belt-buckle, shield-boss and battle axe, Alfgar the great ealdorman himself came riding. All was misted with the steamy sweat and breath of horses in the snow.

'Lord King, God be thanked!' cried Alfgar. He dismounted, and ran toward Alfred. He took both the King's hands. 'Thank God you are safe!'

'Safe and well,' said the King. 'But what of the enemy? Have you news?'

'Nothing had been heard when we left Shaftesbury,' said Alfgar. 'Last night's storm closed all roads. I hope there will be news waiting for us when we get back. I have sent out scouts. Mount, Lord, let us not stay here a moment longer. Food, clothes, news, everything you need is at Shaftesbury. Let us away quickly.'

'Someone take the little girl,' said the King. Escwin lifted Hildis to his saddle.

'These people,' said the King, pointing to the peasants. 'I have nothing here to give them. Have you something?'

The man and the old woman were standing silent in the snow outside the cottage. Behind them in the doorway the wife was looking out. She had come from her bed. The little boy was peeping round from behind her.

Alfgar had brought nothing but his weapons. Nobody had money. Nobody had anything but weapons of war.

'Some bread, perhaps. Has anyone any bread in his wallet?' asked the King. But they could not find a crumb. They had come away in haste.

The King mounted. He turned to the peasant and his family and said:

'I owe you for my lodging, as well as for all the bread I have burned. You shall be repaid within these two days.'

The horses shook their bridles and wheeled about, and all the great company then rode off into the trees, trampling the bright snow under their hooves in the flashing sun. At the cottage door the peasants stood without a word, and watched them out of sight.

CHAPTER TWENTY-THREE

Hostages

EALDORMAN ALFGAR had remained at Shaftesbury with his thanes, to await the King's return. He had not been able to dismiss his uneasiness, though he knew no reason for it. Shaftesbury was a windy and difficult place in the winter. Alfgar's wife complained of the steepness of the slippery hill in the snow, and wished they had gone back two days before, to their more comfortable vill in Cranbourne Chase, as had been intended. Alfgar had the hall windows covered with their frames of ox-hides to keep out the wind and snow, and he lay awake all night. In the morning at six he got from his bed to say his prayers, but he had hardly prostrated himself when there came a banging on the outer gate. He cloaked himself and ran out into the snowy yard where the gatekeepers had let in an armed man on horseback. Alfgar recognized Guntram the Frank. Guntram was bloody all down his leg.

'Not mine,' said Guntram, 'but a traitor's. There has been treachery, lord Alfgar. Pray God the King is safe. He is alone in the forest. For the rest, God knows if they are still alive.'

Alfgar had the war-horn blown through the town while Guntram ate and warmed himself and told his story. He had been all night finding his way. He could get no help in the villages, but the thane at Wincanton had sent a guide with him for the last part of the journey. By daylight and with riders who knew the way he hoped he might be back at Alham in time to save some few lives, or perhaps to avenge them, and to find the King.

Alfgar could not immediately muster more than forty-five men, but these he sent at once with Guntram to seek for the

King and do whatever else they could until greater forces could be found. Guntram rode out again at the ninth hour, without sleep, back towards Alham. Alfgar remained at Shaftesbury mustering more men and hoping against hope the King himself might somehow find his way to the town. Then, well after midday, his hopes were rewarded by the arrival of Escwin. Escwin, too, had had a hard journey of it in the snow, and had lost his way more than once; but he could lead Alfgar directly to the King. Alfgar armed himself, and, with the second party which had been assembling, they set out together, in the late afternoon. But darkness and snow overtook them, with such a blizzard that they had no hope of finding their way, and they were forced to take shelter for the night in a farm, before they had gone very far. They set out again next morning at first light, but the snow in parts was so deep it made slow going, and so they could not reach the King till the sun was high in the sky. But the sun now was as warm as it was bright. They rode back with the King through trees that sprinkled thaw-water like a spring shower.

Guntram and his party meanwhile rode back through Bruton and over the hill towards Alham. They went cautiously, thinking at any moment they would see the heathen war-bands in the fields. But there was no sign of them. Only, among the trees where the Dragon Hall stood, a blue fume of dying smoke lingered. Guntram left the others hidden and went on alone on foot, to see. He found the few last black ribs of the Dragon Hall bending over the smouldering heap like mourners, surrounded by the burnt-out relics of the great hedge. In the clearing the bodies of the dead, both Dane and Saxon, were laid out ready to be buried. But the ground was too frozen for digging. Prayn the reeve with a small party of villagers was preparing to carry the Christian dead back to the houses of the vill for shelter. The heathen they were leaving to the wolves.

Iron-coated Guntram came out from the trees and looked down for the last time upon Britnoth and his friends. He said

'God rest their souls.' Then he asked Prayn where the heathen were, and the reeve told him they had all ridden away northwards again, taking the Atheling with them. And who now was left at the vill? Only the Lady Waltruda and her sons, said the reeve. The Atheling's young wife, with her mother and her brother Beorn, had left that morning. Beorn had taken them back into Mercia, so that Edith could join her husband, wherever he was. As for the Lady Waltruda, she was lamenting for her daughter Hildis, whom she supposed had been lost in the fire at the Dragon Hall, and for her husband, who was killed. Guntram shrugged. He went back to his company, and together they all rode down to the vill.

Waltruda and her two sons were alone in the great stone hall when Guntram entered with his men, their swords drawn. She stood up. She asked: 'What do you want with me?'

'Lady,' said Guntram, 'I do not know what part you have played in all this business and I am not here to take revenge upon you. Your husband I know is dead. That pays part of the debt, but not enough. If King Alfred is dead also, nothing is enough that you or yours can repay. Meanwhile, those two boys there, I take them for hostages.'

'I have lost both my husband and my daughter,' said Waltruda, 'would you take my sons also?'

'The game has its rules,' replied Guntram. 'What did you expect, lady?'

So Elric and Elred were bidden to fetch their great cloaks and mounted their horses and rode away soon after with Guntram's guard. As they went, the serf Howel stood by the courtyard gate. He then went into the hall where the Lady Waltruda sat quite alone.

'Mistress,' he said, 'my master Unferth had promised me my freedom, at the end of my service for him.'

'Take it, Howel,' she said. 'I grant it you. Go and be free.'

'Mistress,' he said, 'what now will you do?' She looked at him wondering why he asked. He went on: 'Now that I can have my freedom at last, it brings no pleasure. Maybe it will be better when I have forgotten what had to be done to earn it. Meanwhile I do not know where to go. You are alone now, mistress. I will stay here still and serve you, if I may.'

She answered: 'As you will, Howel.'

Guntram and the others rode back towards Shaftesbury through the forest by a different path. They found no sign of King Alfred. The snow and darkness which some miles away had driven Alfgar and his party to shelter, now overcame Guntram's men also. They struggled through wild land to Wincanton, and there took shelter for the night. Guntram slept soundly, stiff with fatigue, in his armour.

Next morning in the sunshine they made further searches in the forest before turning again towards Shaftesbury. As they approached the River Stour at the Ecclif bridge they saw ahead of them another company riding the same way. It was Alfgar's party, with the King. They spurred their horses. Thus, joyfully at the bridge they met again, King Alfred with Guntram, and Hildis with her brothers.

CHAPTER TWENTY-FOUR

The Cost of Peace

GUTHORM had been successful beyond even his own expectation. He had caught the West Saxons entirely off their guard. The sudden killing of Ethelhelm had left the Wiltshire men without a leader to whom they could rally, and it was upon Wiltshire that the first brunt of the attack had fallen. Now also was heard the rumour that King Alfred himself had been captured by the heathen, just as Edmund of East Anglia had been captured seven years before, and his body even now was hanging, like that of King Edmund, all stuck with arrows on a tree. The rumour, however false, had time enough in the first few days to do its work. The West Saxons were beginning to lose heart at last. And to add to all this the bad weather hindered communication. Roads were blotted out and made impassable by the snow. When the King returned to Shaftesbury on that second day of the invasion there were no messengers awaiting him, no news from any part of Wessex.

Alfgar had sent a messenger to warn Ethelnoth of Somerset, and had posted scouts out on the Downs as far as Egbert's Stone to watch for the coming of an enemy, if enemy there were; for as yet he knew nothing except that a treacherous attack had been made upon the King. Neither scout nor messenger had yet returned; and now in the sunlit thaw the roads had all been turned into quagmires and running streams.

In the afternoon, after the King had eaten, and put on clean clothes, and while he was making preparations for his return to Winchester, there appeared a party of men riding over the hills from that direction. They came splashing up the road into Shaftesbury. The tall, lean figure in the midst of them was quickly recognized. It was Athelheah, bishop of Sherborne.

The bishop had been at Wilton, near Sarum, when the heathen invaders killed Ethelhelm and raided down to Avon valley to Amesbury. He had seen the people of Wiltshire in flight. He had been with Cetwin the shire-reeve when that brave old man had tried unavailingly to hold Amesbury. Wulfric of Hampshire was said to be mustering a force, a small number, the best that could be done in so short a time; but nothing had yet been seen of it. The bishop had set out for Sherborne, to help prepare the defence of the West Country, as soon as the weather allowed. It was with joy and astonishment, therefore, that now on his way he met the King in Alfgar's hall in Shaftesbury. Then quickly he reported what in these last two days had happened in Wiltshire. The King said: 'We have seen one finger only, not yet the whole hand. I fear there may be worse news to come.'

It came that evening. Messengers riding from Ethelnoth of Somerset, and on their way to Winchester to find the King, came into Shaftesbury and told of the capture of Chippenham, and of the marching of a great pagan army once again in Wessex. The whole hand now began to be seen.

'This must be said, though it will not please you, King Alfred,' said the bishop. He spoke from the torchlit shadows in the darkness of the hall where they sat. 'Do you not now remember my words to you at Exeter? I told you then how the Lord God punished Saul, King of Israel, because of his mercy in sparing the life of Agag the Amalekite. I will pray God he does not punish you as Saul was punished, for your folly in sparing the life of Guthorm, when he was in your power. For depend upon it, this now is Guthorm once again.'

A silence fell. Then King Alfred spoke from out of the shadow where he sat against the wall:

'Lord Bishop, I have thought about this question very often, and it is a hard one to answer. Is it true, as it sometimes seems to be, that cruel brutality will always win every contest, unless it is opposed by a brutality equal to itself? If so, then the things we all seek and admire most in this world, the rule of law, the skills of learning, the builder's craft, the poet's music, the hearth and the cultivated field, all love and loyalty and trust, these we may only enjoy so long as we pay for them in blood and brutality. Our purpose, yours and mine, lord bishop, is to preserve the Christian Church and the lawful heritage of our people here in Wessex. To defend these we have locked our shields together in bloody war, face to face with Guthorm and his like, time after time; and now, shortly, we shall do so yet again. But if we and not Guthorm are to win in the end, surely it must not be because our brutalities are stronger than his, but because our purposes are higher. Surely it is a better thing to be merciful than to be cruel in cold blood. Therefore my heart was against the killing of Guthorm at Exeter, and therefore I spared him.'

'Yet if you had slain him then, Lord King,' said Alfgar, 'he would not now be here again in Wessex, bringing war.'

'Not he, indeed, but some other, sooner or later, having no better example to follow, but only hatred and revenge.' The King paused in thought awhile; then he concluded: 'Lord Bishop, and my friend Alfgar, if it is true that I was wrong in sparing Guthorm's life at Exeter, then it seems the time has now come for me to put the matter right. Now once again I must lead you in war, and with God's help once again we shall win. But in the end once again it will not be by killing but by making peace that things will be put right. We cannot kill all these heathen. We must in the end live as neighbours with them. I promised Guthorm that if he came into Wessex again I would teach him a certain thing, and that promise I will keep.'

The next morning in the grey light before sunrise King Alfred and the bishop mounted their horses in Alfgar's court, and each with his party rode away, the King towards Winchester the bishop to Sherborne. But before they left the dim hall they saw the three children, Elric, Elred and Hildis, asleep on the straw near the hearth.

'These three I leave in your care, lord bishop,' said the King. 'They are the children of Unferth of Alham. I fear Ethelnoth of Somerset will have no love for them. But to the little girl I owe my life, and her brothers may have the makings of good men. Take care of them for me till I return again.'

The mud of the slippery road flew and scattered under the horses' hooves. The King, with Escwin and Guntram the Frank, was in Winchester again that evening. On the way they saw nothing of war. One would have thought the country was still at peace. It was the day of Twelfth Night. In many parts of the country where the new Danish invasion was still a faraway matter, the familiar feast was once again, as every year, being celebrated around cheerful hearths.

In Selwood at a poor peasant's cottage that day there came two riders to the door. They handed over to the old woman there a sack of flour and twelve bread-cakes newly baked, without the least burning. That night when the family went to eat they found in each cake a silver Wessex shilling minted with the head of King Alfred.

King
Alfred.

CHAPTER TWENTY-FIVE

A Plan

KING ALFRED gathered as many of his thanes as could be found in Winchester and held council there. They brought bad news for him from all quarters. The town of Guildford had been plundered and burnt. The thanes in Surrey and Kent were said to be in bad heart, and ready to make any sort of peace with the heathen if they were attacked. The lords of north Wiltshire, in the Vale of Pewsey, where Guthorm's jarls now went unopposed seizing whatever they chose, had fled, leaving their people leaderless. Many had taken ship with their families meaning to settle in France or Lombardy, forsaking Wessex forever. Guthorm ruled from his great camp at Chippenham like the king he claimed to be, and it was said when he divided Wessex to his liking he would put a Saxon king of his own choosing to rule over certain parts of it. Meanwhile, from other parts of England and from overseas, the hungry companies of pagan land-seekers came in to swell his army. They spread out from Chippenham in all directions.

King Alfred asked: 'How long will it be, lords, before we can put an army of Wessex into the field, things being as they are?

They answered: 'For such a war as this, an army of five or six thousand men will be needed at the least. They must all be brought together and fed, and this at a bad time of year when food is scarce and all men are needed on their farms. Still we might do it, though it will take many weeks now, to be truly ready.'

'How many weeks?' the King asked. They answered: 'Perhaps eight, perhaps ten. If it were possible it would be best to wait till spring, with the better marching weather.' But by then, they agreed, the enemy might be settled in such strength that none could dislodge him.

The King looked around him at the council of his lords. Few enough there were of them that day. Wulfric of Hampshire was there, and Cnebba, and Escwin, and Guntram the King's friend. There was also Cetwin, the shire-reeve of Wiltshire, and Bishop Tunbeort of Winchester. But Sigeric of Berkshire was lacking, and the other ealdorman of the eastern shires. This was not the Wessex that had been. The King then spoke as follows:

'Lords, here is a plan:

'First, consider the enemy. He has fixed his base at Chippenham where the country is rich and well provided, since it has not before been touched by war. From there he spreads out and threatens us in every part. But the farther he spreads, the weaker he is at his centre. If this centre is threatened he will pull back his outposts, and we shall have better opportunity to collect our forces.

'Next consider ourselves. We need time, for two reasons; first to mobilize the army, and, second, to recover our old courage and purpose, which, by the suddenness and surprise of his attack, Guthorm has taken from us.

'Therefore my plan is this: I shall myself go to Somerset, and there with Ethelnoth's help, with whatever force we can raise, be it large or small, I will make war upon Guthorm as near to his base as I can, and so keep him busy there. Thus the heathen will not venture too far afield. Meanwhile, in other parts, you shall prepare your people for the fight that is coming. You must be ready to march soon after Easter. Then, when I send you the signal, we will gather at an appointed place and strike. Let us learn from Guthorm about this. We will do as he did: prepare secretly, assemble quickly and strike suddenly. If the enemy does not expect it, when we do strike him at last it will be a final blow which will drive him out of Wessex for ever.

But until then you will have to play the waiting game, while I lie hidden in Somerset. Guthorm shall feel my sting but not know where to find me.'

The thanes agreed to this plan. They thought that by the spring they could gather an army of some five thousand men, from Hampshire and the western shires alone. With things as they were now, they could not count on any help from Kent and the other shires of the east.

It was necessary to appoint a new ealdorman for Wiltshire, in Ethelhelm's place, and the King therefore appointed Edmund, cousin to Ethelhelm, a man of great spirit, strong, black bearded and known for his powerful voice. It was now his task, with Cetwin the Reeve, to rally the Wiltshire people, and wait for Easter.

The King sat that evening with the Lady Elswitha and his children. He had at this time only one son, the Atheling Edward, a lad not yet eight years old. The Atheling sat now with Alfred Dane-Leg the secretary, who was teaching him his letters. Wulfric the ealdorman was with the King also.

'I leave my family in your care for the time being, Wulfric,' said the King. 'If there is any danger, give them an escort to bring them to the west country, to my vill at Sherborne. But otherwise it would be well for them to stay here for the time being. If the King's family is thought to be in flight, others will follow their example. I will send later, nearer the time, and they shall join me.'

Alfred Dane-Leg then rose up, standing with his crutch. 'Lord King,' said he, 'whom will you take with you now, as secretary?'

The King looked at him, a young man who had grown tall in his service. 'Why, I will take you, Namesake,' he said. 'You with your one leg, and I with only half my kingdom, as now it seems; we will see what we can make of things, between the two of us. Be ready to ride at first light tomorrow.'

To the lady Elswitha he said: 'Pray that this will be our last parting, lady. How many battles can you remember?'

She answered: 'Three long campaigns and six great battles, lord. And will this be the last? Well, I will pray so.'

So the King rode at first light, westward again towards Somerset. There went with him his thanes Cnebba and Bracwealla, Alfred his secretary, and Guntram the Frank, and some fifteen others, all brave men of good family. They rode to Somerton where Ethelnoth awaited them.

CHAPTER TWENTY-SIX

Ethelnoth

THE Great Marsh of Somerset reaches for twelve miles back from the sea coast into the middle of the shire. To ride all around it is fifty miles. It follows the course of two rivers which every day when the tide comes up from the sea spill over into the wide fields of sedge all round. In some parts, the Marsh is never dry and the waves ripple over it as on a lake, though often the water is no more than ankle deep. Here, only the people of the Marsh know what channels are fit for a boat to navigate, or where, an inch under the surface, there are causeways firm enough to pass on foot. In other parts during much of the year the Marsh has an appearance of dry land. Thickets of alder grow there, deer and rabbits are seen among the bushes; but only the people of the Marsh know the few paths that are safe for a hunter. Bottomless quagmires lie beneath the soft flowering surface on every side. There only at flood time do the lurking waters rise into view, stretching away among the reeds and bushes to the distant sea.

In the midst of the Marsh there are certain islands of firm ground, most of which can be reached only by boat, though in one place there is a dry causeway partly linking the largest island with the mainland; but even here the river runs between.

At the riverside end of this causeway, guarding the way to the island, a huge grassy mount rises out of the marsh sixty feet high, a fortress built by nature. Here on the summit stood King Alfred with Ethelnoth the ealdorman, one cold winter evening. A red sun descended in the sky, and massy, heroic clouds, all purple, gathered around it. The burning sun glared out from under the clouds across the wide levels of the Marsh, making long and lonely shadows.

'Here is the place,' said Ethelnoth. 'A whole army could live for months here. There is food in plenty, fish and deer and wild fowl, all for the taking. Raiding parties following the marsh paths could strike quickly at any part of the shire. And here, above all, you yourself would be safe from surprise. To my mind it is certain Guthorm has planned to capture you in person. At Alham he attempted it. If he knows already that he has failed, he will try again. You, Lord King, are the heart of Wessex. Here in the Marsh the heart can beat strongly, and be in the front rank of battle and yet be safe.'

The King said: 'Look yonder, Ethelnoth.'

In the far distance to the northeast a smear of dark smoke lay upon the horizon.

'It is this side of Glastonbury,' said Ethelnoth. 'Some great house in Polden. The heathen will burn houses for mere pleasure when they have looted them. Or perhaps the farmer has dared to defend himself. They will burn for spite. But I see from that smoke that they are now venturing further south.'

'Let us go down,' said the King. 'You are right, Ethelnoth. This winter the Marsh shall be my citadel, if not my kingdom. My banner shall be planted up here on the mount. Now let us see about that smoke. We have three hundred men in arms here. It is time we struck a blow.'

They scrambled down the steep side of the mount to where the boats and the King's guard awaited them, and they rowed up river to Langport village on the southern shore of the Marsh. From here it was a short ride to Somerton, the chief town of the Somerset folk. Here they found a crowd of people, men and women and children who had come that afternoon, in flight from the heathen jarls in the north.

Jarl Asbiorn that day had ridden into the Polden hills with one hundred of his men, to scout out the land and to bring back

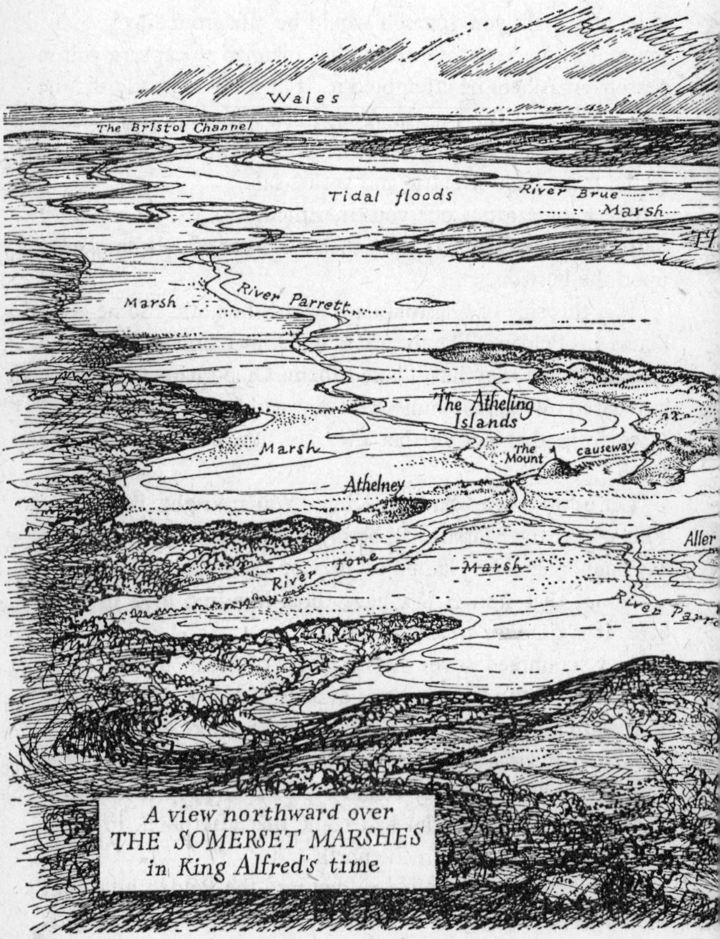

A view northward over THE SOMERSET MARSHES in King Alfred's time

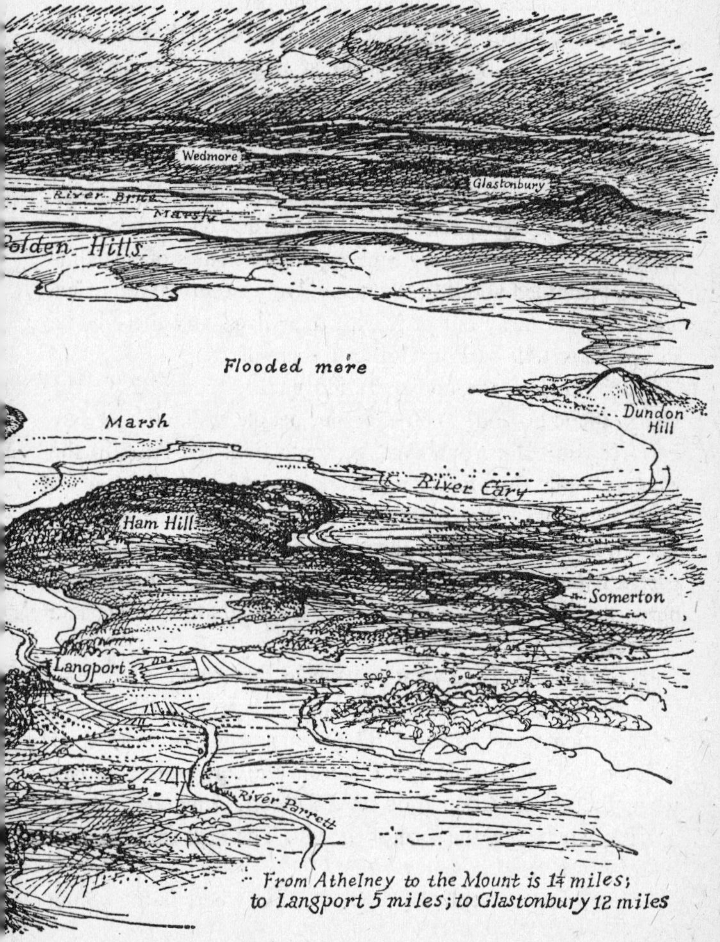

From Athelney to the Mount is 1¼ miles; to Langport 5 miles; to Glastonbury 12 miles

whatever easy wealth he might find on the way. At Walton, near Glastonbury, they found a great store of mead in a thane's house-farm, and some of his men, becoming drunk, ran about with firebrands and burned down every building of the vill, in an orgy of flame and shouting. Jarl Asbiorn laughed loud to see them at it, covered with sweat, running like devils from house to house, flinging everything they could find on to the fires, mad with destruction. They drew off at nightfall, driving their booty of cattle back towards the hills in the north. At a small village, they turned out the people, and sheltered and slept there. Jarl Asbiorn awoke next dawn, hearing a great noise. He ran to the door of the house where he had supped and slept, and there Bracwealla the Saxon struck off his head at a blow. Jarl Asbiorn had no time to see the bodies of his companions tumbled about in the street. Only twenty-seven of his war-band got away out of it with their lives, and these had a sorry tale to tell, back in Guthorm's camp.

Ethelnoth had the bodies buried under a dunghill. To the village thane he said: 'You and your people are no longer safe here. If you value your lives, go south, join the King in the Marshes. The time for village work is over.'

He rode away then with his war party along the ridge of Beacon Hill till he came to the cross-roads where Guthorm had parted from the King the year before. Here Ethelnoth remembered that he was but a mile or two from Alham Vill. He said to Bracwealla:

'We will go and see what remains at that place.'

They rode down into Alham at midday. The vill people were at their work, as usual. The women came out with their distaffs, and the men looked out from the forge and the byre when the armed troop rode in. Ethelnoth demanded of the nearest, where was the lord of the vill. The man said the lord Unferth was dead.

'That I know,' replied Ethelnoth, 'but where is the young lord Edgar?'

The man did not answer; but at the brew-house door the Lady Waltruda appeared, with Prayn the reeve. They were going the round of the estate, taking stock of the year's work and wealth.

'The Atheling is not here,' said the lady: 'I will speak for him. I am Waltruda.'

'What has any of it to do with you, woman?' said Ethelnoth. 'It is not your place. Since the Atheling is not here I claim it for the King. Good men have died here from treachery, and there is a heavy blood-price to be paid to their families. This vill and its people may serve to pay it. As for yourself, since it is none of your business, you may keep the clothes you have on, and go.'

She stood a moment in pale silence, then laid down her distaff. She asked: 'May I fetch a warmer mantle?' Ethelnoth nodded.

She went to her bower, while the horses of the armed men stamped in the silence outside. She came out soon, wrapped in a thick mantle of grey wool. She said nothing, but walked out alone on the path that once led to the Dragon Hall. When she reached the clearing and came in sight of the black ruin she stopped, hearing footsteps behind her. She turned and looked back. It was the serf, Howel.

'Go on, lady,' said he, 'and I will follow you. You cannot go alone.'

So she went on without a word, and he followed.

Two days later Guthorm sent a strong raiding party down the Roman road into Selwood to take revenge for Asbiorn's killing. Ethelnoth had expected it. He had been reinforced at Alham, and had now nearly two hundred men with him. He rode out with them on to Ditcheat Hill, and watched the Danes coming from a distance. He moved off then, and followed the raiders, keeping distant about a mile to one side of them, going along the forest. The Danes were watching him, and presently stopped, as if undecided what to do. Their force was of about the same size, but they could not know how many more Saxons there might be, unseen in the woods. They turned, therefore, and rode back again the way they had come, going a little faster. They skirted a small wood rather than go through, but this did not save them from the flight of arrows that came from it. They lost only one man and three horses by it, but it hastened still more the speed of their going. They ventured back again a little way that night and burned a farm. Neither side had fought a battle, but the Saxons had had the better of the day.

CHAPTER TWENTY-SEVEN

The Marsh King

KING GUTHORM had a great chair which he had taken from the church at Bradford. It was a chair which only bishops had sat in before him. It had a high back with two winged angels carved on it, in attitudes of blessing. It was gilded and painted and had a cushion covered in blue silk. This chair was carried and set down wherever Guthorm went, and none spoke till he was seated in it. Olaf the Skald says that his appearance was very fine though he was not a tall man. He dressed always in coloured clothes with much embroidery, with many arm-rings and necklaces, and rings in his ears. His red beard which he had used to cut short he now grew long, from vanity, because on his head he was growing bald. He greased his head frequently with pig's fat, and wrapped it round every night with horse-hair from a stallion's tail, which he had been told would make the hair grow; but this had little effect. Therefore now he always wore a cap. He suffered much from tooth-ache.

Guthorm sat scowling in his chair in Chippenham church, where he had set up his three gods on the altar as he had promised them. King Alfred's cloak lay in front of them. They grinned at Guthorm in their usual way while he listened to the news from Somerset and scowled. His chieftains sat ranged on each side of him on benches down the church.

'What forces have they there?' he demanded. 'Some few local shire-levies, led by village thanes. None but a king can bring an army together, and hold it together in battle. They have no king till we give them King Edgar, on our terms. These local bands are nothing. Hang them all. There are enough trees in Selwood.'

'They speak of a king,' said Einar, from his place.

'A fine one you are to tell me such things,' said Guthorm. 'You listen to woman's talk. I sent you to make havoc in Selwood, after Asbiorn's death. Asbiorn was my friend, and he was killed by a band of Wessex churls. And you come creeping back without spilling blood, telling me of kings and armies. What king and where?'

'Mock as you will, but it is true,' Einar answered, hotly. 'What king I cannot tell you. But they say certainly there is a king, and that he has set up his standard in the Great Marsh.'

Guthorm roared with laughter, rocking backwards and forwards in his chair.

'In the Marsh!' he mocked. 'A Marsh King! Dirty Foot, King of Mud!'

Einar, red with anger, sprang to his feet.

'Laugh, then, King Guthorm,' he said, 'but will you dare call me a coward? I will fight against the odds where need be, though I would prefer to have them on my side. But I tell you I will not fight at all when I do not know what the odds are, one way or another. First find out, Guthorm. The Marsh may be deeper than you think.'

Guthorm growled at him: 'I know you are no coward, Einar. Very well, let us find out more about this Marsh King.'

Einar, being angry, refused to go again into Selwood until others had gone and come back to confirm his statement. Jarl Torgils Auk therefore set out some days later with a strong company, and rode south till he came to the downland by Ethandune. Here on the steep hillside is the image of a great horse, cut into the chalk, and above it on the hill's edge is an ancient rampart, looking out over the forest. These forts and ramparts, like the dead bodies of old wars, lie all along the westward edge of the Down. Torgils stayed below, in the forest. He came to a number of villages but saw none but peasants working their lands. He saw no fighting men. At the Roman road he turned westward and, passing near Alham, came at the end of his second day's journey to the northern regions of the Marsh near Glastonbury. By chance they came to the village where Asbiorn had died, and the people fled, seeing them. Torgils caught a number of the men and roped them together and demanded to know where the lord of the district was to be found. When they did not answer he whipped them until they told him. They said he had gone with a number of his men to join the ealdorman and the King. They had taken a boat and gone out over the Marsh.

'And is that where they think they will find the King?' asked Torgils. The men said yes.

'What king?' demanded Torgils. 'Who is he?'

'Why,' said they, 'King Alfred. Who else could it be, lord?'

'What liars they are! Let them all hang!' shouted Torgils, and he rode away in anger. But next day he had similar answers from others along the marshside. He hanged them also. 'It cannot be!' he said aloud to himself repeatedly, as later he rode back with his men to Chippenham. He began to have doubts about his night attack at Alham. Who had that man been, the one who had ridden away? He was glad, when he got back to Chippenham, to find that King Guthorm was not there.

Guthorm had ridden to Bristow. He had had a message from old Hubba, who had put in there with some of his ships. Guthorm found Hubba living aboard ship, under the tent.

'You have become a big sort of fellow now,' said Hubba.

'Big enough to get up again, after I have been down,' said Guthorm. 'What about you, in this way?'

'I am big enough to know my limit,' said Hubba. 'Besides, I am older than you. The thing I fear is that I shall grow tired of it all. Before that happens I mean to put my oar in again. I told you I would be your jackal if you proved to be a good lion. You are good enough, anyway. Let me come in on it.'

'Have you still your twelve ships?' Guthorm asked him.

'I have three and twenty,' said Hubba. 'You are not the only one to improve his fortunes.'

They filled a horn, therefore, and drank to their better fortunes.

'Old friend,' said Guthorm, 'this is the way I want it. You know the Somerset flats, where the river marshes are. Those marshes may be a danger to us. They tell me there are fighting men there. If so I mean that they should stay there, and not come out. We should take the land all round them, therefore. I will take all on this side; you take the other. South of the Marsh is all the best land of Somerset. We will divide it between us. There, and all to the west of it is yours.'

'The Devon people may have something to say about that,' said Hubba, 'but I can deal with them.'

So they exchanged gifts and parted. Hubba then called his ship-boy to bring him a canvas bag he kept under the stern lifting. Opening this he pulled out from it a great flag. He unrolled it and then unfolded it three times, and spread it out athwart the ship. It was the Raven Banner of the three sons of Ragnar, Hubba, Ingvar and Halfdan. Their three sisters had woven the black raven on it, many long years ago. This was the famous banner whose raven was said to dance and flutter in the flag before a victory, but would hang down motionless if a defeat was likely. It had seen a world full of victories over a long lifetime. Ingvar and Halfdan were now dead. Only Hubba remained.

'Once more for a last fight, then, old banner,' said he. 'Up you go on the pole.'

The ship rocked at its moorings and the halyards flapped against the mast in the evening breeze. The vikings saw the raven banner shaking out on its pole, and they came aboard the ship with high hearts, and rowed Hubba back down the river to rejoin his fleet.

Back in Chippenham camp Guthorm sought for Torgils.

He found he had been back, but had ridden away again. Guthorm cursed.

'He should have waited. I want news of this Marsh King. Did he say nothing?'

Einar said: 'Only that there is a king of some sort, as I told you.'

Torgils came into the camp again some days later and found Guthorm biting his nails and spitting the pieces out.

'You have been a long time about it,' said Guthorm. 'So now, who is this famous Marsh King? What is his name, what is his strength, what have we to do about him?'

'It is nothing worth trouble, King Guthorm,' Torgils answered. 'A local chieftain whom you will snuff out without difficulty. I did not learn his name.'

CHAPTER TWENTY-EIGHT

The Stronghold

ODDA, Ealdorman of Devonshire, was a small man, very sinewy and ugly, and he rode a small and ugly horse. He came riding down from the moors of north Devon on a windy day in February, into Somerset country, along the western side of the Marsh. He had twelve of his servants with him, well armed. In Taunton village a guide awaited him, from the King. The guide led the way eastward beyond the Taunton fields into thin woods of alder, and beyond these again on to a tongue of land from which the trees had all been cleared away, giving a view out over the marshland on either side. At the far end of this peninsula the land dipped down into a channel of marsh which separated it from a low island beyond. Two short, wooden bridges, covering the boggy parts of the channel, completed a firm but muddy road between the peninsula and the island, where a stockade of rough-hewn timber with a gate and a watch-tower blocked the way. Here the ealdorman's party was challenged. The gate was opened, and they passed through.

All over the island a camp village of huts was being built among the trees. The huts were grouped into colonies, but there was little to distinguish one rough, reed-thatched building from the next. At the centre of the camp, however, with an open assembly-space before it, there were two huts together, surrounded by a stockade, and at the entry to this stood the King's flag on its pole. Here there were a number of the King's thanes whom Odda knew. The King's young secretary, the Dane-Leg, was among them. They told him the King was not there, but was over on the great island beyond, and likely to be away till nightfall. Ealdorman Ethelnoth was with him, they said. Odda therefore decided to follow, and went on, with one of the King's thanes for guide, leaving his men and his horses. There was a rough causeway leading from the island to the river, where a bridge was being prepared; but this was not yet built and a ferry boat was kept there. On the far side was the great Mount and another causeway over low ground to the main island. In flood time, which would be soon, only the causeway showed above the water. At the island end of it there was a village of the marsh people, who were hunters and fishermen. The large island beyond was all wild and wooded.

They went towards the middle of the large island, and here the King's thane put a horn to his mouth and blew. The horn-call was answered from a distance, and they followed in that direction, till by repeating the horn-calls they came out into the far shore of the island, which looks out over two miles of the Marsh Lake to the hills of Polden, beyond. Here was the King, with Ethelnoth and a company of men. There was a great number of small marsh boats, hidden among the rushes. The King was dressed like a workman, and had mud on his feet and leggings. He greeted Odda as an old friend. They had not met since Exeter, when Odda had departed in anger because of the King's leniency.

'I hope you have not come to chide me, Odda,' said the King.

'No, lord, I have come to warn you,' Odda replied. 'You have a good stronghold here in this bog. I hope very much the heathen swine will try and get at you here. I would be glad to see them sink. I would give them a push down. But what if they come in, not from the land but from the sea?'

'They would have a hard time finding the way,' said Ethelnoth. 'The river's course is lost in marshes all the way from here to the sea flats. They would not attempt it.'

'They are up to something, however,' said Odda. 'I have seen much coming and going of ships over on the Welsh side of the sea. From my high cliffs you can see far. It is not usual for the heathen to bring out their ships at this time of year.'

The King said: 'They could land on your coast, could they not, Odda, and carry war into Devonshire down my western flank, as Guthorm is doing on the eastern side, in Somerset and Wiltshire. This would hem me in. I will soon have a great army here, with God's help, but I shall not be able to use it to best advantage, facing both ways at once. Have you soldiers enough to hold off a landing, if they come?'

'There are not many landing places on that coast,' said Odda 'and I have enough men there to garrison the forts that watch them. But my people are scattered over long distances with great empty moors between. I cannot raise the whole Devonshire army in a moment.'

'I will send you what help I can from here,' said the King.

But Odda replied: 'I will manage it on my own, King Alfred. Never fear, they shall not get by me. And if I have some little chance to show them any mercy,' he added, savagely, 'that chance I will not take.'

The King made no reply to this, knowing Odda's mind. Instead, he showed him the preparations he was making to land raiding parties across the lake, in Polden, from where they could quickly strike at the enemy if they should try to march forces down the Roman road to Somerton and Ilchester. With a fleet of small boats and the marshmen's knowledge of the channels they could strike at will at any point around the Marsh, especially along the eastern borders between Somerton and Glastonbury, where the greatest danger was. Ethelnoth had occupied the ancient fortress on Dundon Hill, and had set a great fire-stack ready there, to give warning all over the lake if the pagans came down that way.

It was beginning to rain when in the evening they all went back across the river to the smaller island. The whole place was very bleak and grey. It was still raining next morning when Odda departed, and pools were oozing up all over the Marsh. He went back to the coast on the borders of Devon and Somerset, where he had a fortress just over a mile inland from the sea. The place is called Kynwit. It stands on a high steep hill, very sheer all round except towards the east, where the path comes up from the beaches. From Kynwit Odda could watch the whole coastline eastwards, all the way to the marsh flats at the river mouth. Westwards the cliffs rose up with very few beaches. By Odda's reckoning the beaches near Kynwit would be the most likely place for any landing aimed at King Alfred in his marsh fortress. He sent word to all his thanes in the region to muster their fighting men and gather at Kynwit. Six hundred men he gathered there. At other places along the coast also he had men ready; but here he gathered the most.

A rough stone rampart surrounded Kynwit fort. The yard within was huddled with huts. The round shields hung clustered on every wall. The sharp spears stood together at every doorway. The grindstones were busy with swords and axes. The rainy weather did not cool Odda's hot mood, and he cursed the low sweeping clouds that hid the sea.

In the Great Marsh the rivers swelled, the pools became lakes. The King in his island still had no news from the men of Wiltshire or beyond. Alfgar sent no word of the Dorset men. But from the north of Somerset every day there came those who had been driven from their lands by the heathen, and now were making their way to the King in the marshes, or to Ethelnoth in Somerton. The blacksmiths were kept busy hammering out spear heads. The fields that year were ploughed with wooden plough-shares, for the iron shodding had all been taken to make weapons.

Ethelnoth learned one day that Einar the Jarl had once more brought a great body of heathen into Selwood, and had set his camp at Froom. Soon after this Prayn, the vill-reeve, with many of the people of Alham, among them being Rotri the smith and Penda the falconer, Duri's father, came to Ethelnoth at Somerton. The ealdorman frowned to see them, for he was unwilling to forgive the name of Alham, but he could find no fault in these men for themselves. They told him that the heathen had set up a watch post on the hill above Alham, and that the people had fled from their houses. Grudgingly, therefore, Ethelnoth let them stay in the camp he had set up for those who fled to him from the heathen.

But Ethelnoth marched to Alham by night with sixty men. He surprised the Danes at their watch post, and those sleeping in the vill, and drove them out with great slaughter. His men set fire to the roof of the hall and it burned all night and did not fall till broad daylight. The stone walls remained. Ethelnoth left a desert, which had once been a king's mansion. He had lost only two men killed, and returned with all the rest to the marshland.

CHAPTER TWENTY-NINE

The Convent

DURING all those early weeks of the year, while the King in his marsh fortress was watching and waiting and gathering his forces for the spring, Hildis and her brothers remained with the household of Ealdorman Alfgar at Shaftesbury. Bishop Athelheah, though the King had put them in his charge, had passed on the care of them to Alfgar for the time being. He said to Alfgar and Bertha, Alfgar's wife:

'It is more fitting the boys should stay with you and learn the business of manhood along with your own sons, until the King decides what shall be done with them. As for the girl, that is another matter. I shall advise the King that later on she should enter a house of nuns. There is no better life for a woman. Meanwhile she can live and learn at the convent of St. Cuthberga. The nuns there need all the help they can get. Every day there are more refugees coming from the north; the infirmary is never empty, and many of the nuns are old. I will send my chaplain to arrange about it.'

Hildis wept when they told her of the bishop's decision. She did not wish to be parted from her brothers. But Alfgar said sternly:

'Girl, you cannot stay with your brothers always. In any case, in a few days they must come away with me into the shire. And the bishop is right. A convent life is most suitable for a woman. Many of the ladies of St Cuthberga's are of noble kindred. What better could you ask?'

The convent was situated in a river valley not far from Shaftesbury, at a place called Donhead. The nuns had come there only two years before, from their house at Wimborne, which had been sacked and burned by the Danes during the warfare in Dorset. The nuns, having themselves been refugees from the fury of the heathen, could not now fail to have compassion for all these new victims of the enemy. Many sick and old people had fled with their families, and some of these, failing and ailing by the roadside, had made their way to St Cuthberga's. But there was no room for their families to stay with them, even though they could have helped with the work of the convent and its farm.

Hildis was taken to the convent and there put into the charge of Sister Deodeda, the old nun who looked after the infirmary. The infirmary had once consisted only of one building outside the convent enclosure, but it had now been extended by taking over some of the smaller farm buildings nearby. Some of the female serfs had been brought from their farm work to help Sister Deodeda and the other nuns in the infirmary. Hildis, from the moment she entered this new life, was kept so hard at work she had little time to be sad. The nuns were not unkind to her, and being young, and with all her hard work, she was not expected to follow the whole of the austere life to which the convent sisters daily devoted themselves. She was not called from her sleep to say the Office in the dark middle of the night, nor did she have to spend more than an hour each morning and evening at prayers in the chapel. She pitied the poor nuns who had to spend so long at their devotions in the shivering cold, their fingers and toes all red and swollen with chilblains. When she prayed she found herself often praying that such a life should not be hers. She wept often at night, dreaming, both waking and sleeping, of all that had so suddenly been taken away from her, of Alham, of her mother whom she feared she now might never see again, of her brothers from whom she had now again been separated, of her father, who, they had told her, had been killed; and then, again and again, of Duri, the falconer's son. She dreamed of him as she had last seen him, covered with blood and snow. She awoke in the night, crying out 'Duri, Duri!' Sister Deodeda, returning from the chapel to her bed in a corner of the infirmary heard the cries and came over to where Hildis lay. She said:

'What is the matter? What is this Duri? Pray to God, and He will protect you from all such devils. Get out of bed and pray!'

But Hildis only wept. The old nun did her best to comfort her. Then she said: 'Come now, work is the best cure, next to prayer. Since you will not pray, get you up on your feet and work. It is nearly day already. I must sleep an hour before I turn to; but you can start and mend the fire and heat the water and make things ready. Up now!'

So Hildis wrapped her mantle around her and went out into the yard to fetch logs from the pile. She had a great wicker basket, with wooden rails under it, which she dragged along behind her by a rope, like a sledge, and this she began to fill with the logs. But the logs were all frozen together, and they were so big and heavy she could not separate them. While she was pulling at them, suddenly from behind the woodpile the figure of a man rose up. He was wrapped up in his cloak and had a sack over his head and shoulders, tied round his neck to keep it together. Hildis cried out in fright at this shadowy apparition. But the man said:

'Do not be frightened. I pray you, let me help with the logs and come in by the fire. I am cold.'

He began stiffly to separate the logs from the pile, and so together they filled the basket and dragged it into the dark house. They raked together the embers of the fire which soon began to glow and crackle, and they put on the small pieces and twigs lopped from the bigger logs till soon the welcome fire began to blaze and throw its light, showing the huddled sleepers all along the wall. The man crouched warming himself by the fire, and Hildis for the first time saw his face in the light, and recognized him.

'Howel!' she cried, 'It is you!'

It was he indeed. He saw and recognized her in his turn. He began to laugh in a stupid manner.

'Ah, Lady Hildis,' he said, 'this is a miracle. Your mother has thought you were lost or dead; she has mourned for you. What has happened to you, lady, where have you been? It is a miracle!'

'But, Howel, what brings you here? What has happened at home? Is my mother well?'

'Lady, she is here now. Come with me, quickly.'

He led her out across the yard to a shed on the far side, against the fence. He moved aside the hurdle which closed the doorway. He had to bend down to look in.

'Waken, lady,' he said. 'Waken, for here is your daughter, the Lady Hildis.'

Waltruda, huddled within, in her grey mantle, sat up in the straw and faintly by the thin light of dawn she saw Hildis peeping in at the door. She thought she must still be dreaming, but Hildis came in, feeling her way in the darkness inside the shed, to her mother. They clasped each other tightly. Waltruda said:

'Hildis, my baby, what has happened to you?' So until it was full daylight they sat together telling what had befallen them, while Howel sat outside by the doorway. Over in the convent enclosure the clapper was beating to call the nuns to Prime, and Sister Deodeda at the infirmary door was calling for Hildis. Hildis said to her mother:

'Come with me, come into the warm. But oh, my mother, I do not wish to stay here and become a nun.'

Waltruda said: 'We must do now whatever God puts to our hand, whether we wish to or no. But if you stay here I will stay also, if the Mother Abbess will allow me.'

So they went first to Sister Deodeda and told her what had come about, and the old nun beat her knuckles against her forehead and said: 'So many people and always so good a reason! What can we do, how are we to feed them all?'

But the Mother Abbess gave permission for Waltruda to stay

during the whole season of Lent, to be near her daughter, and Howel lived with the serfs of the farm and worked there. Elric and Elred could not yet be told about their mother, because they had already gone with Alfgar into the shire, where the men of Dorset were sharpening their weapons, and oiling the wood of their shields and the leather of their hauberks, ready for the day that was soon to come.

CHAPTER THIRTY

Island of Princes

THE Great Marsh was now all water, a continuous lake in which, except for a few trees and bushes here and there standing lonely in their own reflections, only King Alfred's islands, with the Mount and the causeway, showed above the surface. The floods had for a time put a stop to all work on the bridge and so the journey between the smaller and the greater island had still to be made by boat. The King and his company therefore remained on the smaller island. The way across to the peninsula, though it was not submerged, was little more than ankle deep in most places and could be waded. The path was marked out by stakes linked with a rope. Hither came Alfgar one evening with a mounted troop. With him also came two thanes of Wiltshire and Hampshire. Their names were Denwald and Sithgar. They came with news for the King. He came himself to the gate to welcome them, and they greeted him with great joy. It seemed that without him the land of Wessex had fallen apart.

As they went through the camp to the King's house they saw all men busy at their trades. Thanes and their servants together shod the horses and felled the trees. The smoke of the forge fires blew all about, for it was a windy evening. A smell of baking bread came from one of the huts as they passed, and a man was running back hurriedly from outside. They heard his voice shouting angrily within:

'Fool of a boy, what were you dreaming of? Had I not come back in time they would all have been burned to a cinder!'

The King stopped a moment and smiled suddenly. Alfgar said to him:

'Why do you smile, King Alfred? I've had my ears boxed often enough for the same reason when I was a lad, out hunting with my father.'

'You, too, Alfgar?' asked the King.

'Indeed, yes, lord. If you don't keep turning the batch, they'll be all afire before you can say knife. You have to keep a close eye on it.'

The King laughed. 'Indeed I have found it so,' he said.

They went on to the King's hearth within the palisade, where Guntram the Frank and Cnebba the King's thane awaited them. The young Alfred Dane-Leg stood by his writing table. The King bade all be seated. Food and drink was brought to them. He passed the ale-horn among them, himself drinking a sip first and last, in token of welcome. He then asked what news they had brought from the Shires.

Denwald spoke first:

'I bring greetings from Ealdorman Edmund and the Wiltshire men, King Alfred. We have suffered much and lost great lands and many kindred. Yet we have found our heart again if ever we lost it. Because the enemy is so much in the midst of us we shall find it hard to raise our greatest number, but every man who comes will come to fight as two. We reckon ourselves a force of nine hundred men. This you may count upon. There may be more when the day comes.'

Sithgar then said:

'The lord Wulfric sends greetings to King Alfred. We of Hampshire can muster a thousand. There will be more in April, if matters can wait till then. But the ploughing and sowing will not wait. When these are done you need only name the day and the place.'

'I, too, shall bring my thousand,' said Alfgar, 'or more when Easter is past. But name the day when you will, King Alfred. We will be there.'

'Guthorm has five thousand on land, at the least,' said the King, 'and it is thought he has another sea-army at his call.

Odda of Devonshire is watching the coast for them. Until I know which way that cat will jump I cannot be sure either of day or place. I must wait for that, and I must still wait a little for your own strengths to grow. Half-measures will not do. When the day comes for me to send out the war-signal, Guthorm and his mob shall be made to give back to Christ every ounce of blood and treasure that they owe. This let us be sure of.'

'Appoint now what you will send, for a war-signal,' said Sithgar, 'so when it comes we shall know it comes from you only.'

The King thought for a moment, then, rising, he went to the table and took a loaf of bread. He thrust this into the fire on the end of his sword, and held it there until it was charred black all over. Then he drew it out, and when it was cool he broke it into three pieces, and gave a piece to each of the shire men.

'Burnt bread is the King's sign,' said he. 'When this comes, it is for Guthorm's reckoning. Alfgar, be ready to turn the batch.'

Later that evening, when the other matters had been settled, Alfgar spoke of Waltruda's children. He said that the boys showed well enough in their conduct, and that in his view the elder one was grown enough to march as a soldier. Many a lad of his sixteen years did so. The King agreed. 'But,' he said, 'it is a matter for Guntram here to decide. He knows who killed Unferth, their father. What of his children, Guntram? Will they hold feud with Unferth's killer, do you think, when they are grown men?'

'Will you yourself hold feud with these children, lord, for their father's sake?' Guntram replied. 'Let it be forgotten what they owe you for their father's fault, let them now repay in loyal service. As for Unferth's killer, he can look after himself, I dare say.'

'And the girl, what of her, Alfgar?' asked the King.

Alfgar told what had happened to Hildis.

'The bishop means very well,' said the King, 'but I will see the child myself, before she is committed to a religious life. I, too, owe a debt, and I will see to it that the girl has at least a little part in choosing her own future. The truth is, few of us get so much. I will send for her when the time comes. Write it down, Namesake,' he said to his secretary. 'It is not to be forgotten.'

The wind of the day had blown itself out, except in the higher regions above the earth where clouds like twisted dragons hurried across the white face of the moon. All about the island the marsh lake rippled in the moonlight. By the sedges, looking out over the moonpath of water, stood Denwald with Guntram the Frank.

'Has it a name, this island?' Denwald asked.

'None till now,' said Guntram; 'but since the King and his lords came here they do call it Athelney, or the Atheling Island.'

'Island of Princes, the Ship of Wessex, sailing the flood,' said Denwald. 'Watching the clouds passing overhead, it feels as if the whole island is moving like a ship. God send us a good voyage.'

CHAPTER THIRTY-ONE

The Battle of Kynwit

BRIGHTLY the moon path shone upon the sea, widely seen from high Kynwit wall, the stone fortress where Odda, Helmund's stark son, stood watching. Hands gripping stone wall stood he there proudly. As a ship's prow the wall was to him. Moon-swimming clouds above him breasted the sky, and he felt the fortress as a ship moving, travelling the shadowed sea.

On the dark sea eastward no ship moved that he saw. On the high sea-cliff westward no warning watchfire gleamed. Men slept in Odda's hall, the clustered shields slept on the long walls, weary with waiting. Odda therefore went weary likewise to his bedplace. The sentry alone now on the high wall watched nothing, saw nothing but the crowding shadows of clouds on the face of the moon-gleaming sea. On the high sea-cliff by the watchfire the sentry slept, and did not see the dark ships creeping that way, close below the cliff.

Thus stealthily with silent sail on the rolling waves, unseen, without any warning given, old Hubba the Viking, last of fierce Ragnar's sons, stole like a thief to his last landfall. Three and twenty were his long ships, heavy with murderous men. Swift as eagles they turned their beaks to the beaches, breaking the waves as they came.

One fire half alight on the beach there, three men half awake in the warm of it saw suddenly the shine of the wet prow, heard suddenly the cries of the vikings and the beaching of boats in the breaking surf. They fled fast, taking only their weapons, leaving cloak and shield for first spoils to the plunderer. One man, the slowest, fell dying, fledged with arrows. One other, leg-wounded, crept as best he could into bushes. Only the third on the high hill climbing came to Kynwit. The sleepy sentry heard his call at last, saw then the long ships below on the beaches, the moonlit sails on the sea. Then the hoarse-voiced warning horn, the bull-bellower, he put to his lips and blew, and the fierce Odda, Helmund's son, leaped from his bed and ran before all others to the wall.

He counted the man-carrying boats, the swarming sails below on the long beaches. 'A thousand men if a man they have there, and we here, sleeping, less than six hundred. Shame on us now after this weary while to be found wanting. Now only sinew shall save us, the stark mood of the heart shall be battle's buckler. Let every man prepare to render the grim gift of his life's blood. Not more for our fault shall the King's cause falter.' So on the stony crest of Kynwit they put on the iron mail, bristled the wall with sharp spears.

But below on the boat-laden beach, as old Hubba the Viking stood amid his gathering ranks, a chill finger of something he knew not worked like a worm in his spine. There came thus upon him then the grey knowledge of the sons of Ragnar, he and his brothers, to know instantly the hour of their own death. Thus with his brothers had it boded; so boded it now with him, though he gave it small heed. He bade his men bring the banner, the black raven woven by Ragnar's daughters. The pole of it struck he upright in the soft sand. Wind was there enough to ruffle the raven, to make it shake its wings, the bringer of victory; yet this it did not. Unmoving it hung there listless, clinging close to the pole, a doleful portent. Yet Hubba cried: 'Pack away, then, the black banner. We need not rags to lead us. Forward the war-horn and the stark spear-wall. Great gain awaits us in King Alfred's land.' Yet even as he spoke he felt still the thin worm in his backbone, and he knew that for him no gain of gold awaited.

Those in the vanguard saw then the Saxon host high on the hill of Kynwit. This they told to King Hubba. 'A woeful wall

have they there to hold,' said he. 'On that high hilltop none can come or go, to attack or defend it, but by this one pathway only. Here let us stay, not wasting our work, but waiting. There let them weaken without food or water. Our strength for other foes we will foster.' So they beset the fortress of Kynwit, closing the pathway with their dark ranks, as the ranked clouds closed over the setting moon, and hid with darkness the sea and the beached boats.

Then on the high hilltop Odda the ealdorman spoke to his soldiers. Grim were they in their war-gear. Grim were the words he spoke to them. 'No good shall we gain now by waiting to win this war. Hope have we none for happiness but by blood and blade. Let us out, therefore, and down upon them with dawn's light. Let no man live out this day knowing the pagans have seen the sunrise.' So they came out from the fort, and ranked themselves shield to shield, each man eager for the weapon storm. They went in their ranks down the hill. Odda the fierce lord led them. No word was spoken. So in the pale mist of dawn's undarkening the pagans saw before them suddenly the stark ranks of the Saxons, their deadliest foe.

Now the sound of the trumpet, the horn-call, the loud shouting, now the blood spouting, now the death-dealing blade-blow, the axe-head hacked from the helve in the cleaving, the red way cleft in the splintering shield wall. Odda is first through, striking straight to the bone, red from head to foot with glittering blood. What now shall sunrise show to the heathen host, those that survive the grey dawn and the grim Saxons? What now shall old Hubba see, standing alone in the bowstorm of arrows, the cold worm in his spine's marrow? He shall see red Odda coming, the axe red in his hand. He shall see the end of his life's plundering, his own life plundered. The axe now had found him. He has not seen the sunrise.

Now the red sun rising shone with sharp rays like fire over the fell field. Bodies burned in his light. Heap upon heap lay the foul foe under hacked helmet, under broken buckler. Back to the beach and the ships in full flight headlong ran the remainder, knowing no mercy followed on the sharp swords of the Saxons. 'Kill every man. Let none live!' loudly shouted Odda the fierce fighter. On a shield they carried him forward, woefully wounded. Stricken with sword upon sinew, never more in this life shall he stand upright. Yet still went he forward shield-borne to the front of the battle, sparing none in his wrath.

One thousand men and two hundred they slew there. Field, foreshore and hillside were thick with their bodies. Few indeed were the oarsmen, few the long ships that fled away from that fell shore on the falling tide. Save for these few all were a spoil to the Saxons. Great store of plunder they had there, ship and sail, gold and silver and war-gear.

Now the fair sun of cloudless day shone full on the triumphing Christians. In Hubba's ship they found the abandoned flag, the raven banner of Ragnar. This trophy they brought forth to brave Helmund's son, throned on his shield. 'Thus,' he cried, 'thus have we clipped the wings of the heathen. This send we now to King Alfred as gift of our glory. Say this to the King, that Odda the ealdorman sends him one arm of his enemy, a savage gift of the battle. Better shall come later by other means, maybe. This part is my portion. Let all men know it.'

CHAPTER THIRTY-TWO

Easter at Athelney

THEY brought the raven flag to Alfred in Athelney. They spread it on the ground before him and said: 'Odda sends you this, that you may set your foot upon your enemy. But he, as is only right, has been the first to stand upon it, we helping him. He can never more stand by his own strength. The sinew of his leg is cut. Yonder stain is his blood.'

So the King set his foot on the flag of the foeman and said: 'This gift from Odda, and the gift of his sinew, I receive gratefully and with honour. Say to Odda, that what he has begun, I will firmly finish. It shall not be long.'

It was Ash Wednesday. Bishop Athelheah of Sherborne was with the King in the island, and all who were there had been sprinkled by him with the ashes of penitence. The King said that he would observe the Easter festival here in the Marsh, with his company. Then, when Easter was past, and with the floods going down, they would be able to finish building the bridge and occupy the great island. Then there would be room for a great army that could hold out and harry the heathen for as long as need be, until the shire armies were ready, and the whole power of Wessex could take the field.

The heathen banner was folded up and given to the King, who took it back with him to his house. The bishop went with him. There was a book open on a table, from which the King's secretary was copying certain passages. The bishop was surprised that the King should have brought such a valuable thing with him into such harsh surroundings.

'Would they not be more harsh without it?' asked the King. 'Besides, how can we be sure that there will ever again be a life that is fit for such things, if we do not value them enough to want to keep them with us, even in harsh places? However, the time has come for me to put my book aside for a while, once again.'

So saying, he closed it. The bishop said:

'Five thousand men at the beginning of May. This we now know can be raised from the neighbouring shires.'

'It will be enough,' said the King.

On Good Friday the King went from Athelney three miles by boat over the Marsh to Aller, a small island where, a hundred years before, a colony of monks from Glastonbury had built a church. They had built it of stone from the quarry of Ham Hill, on the mainland nearby. It was a small building, long abandoned by the monks and served now by an old priest who lived there alone. Since he had come to the Marsh, King Alfred had had the church repaired, and now he used it as his own chapel. All Good Friday he spent there, fasting. He fasted still on the following day, though he went over by boat in the evening to the Mount, on the summit of which a great firestack had been built of brushwood. There on the top of the stack the King planted the raven flag of the heathen, and in the first hour of Easter morning he and the bishop together set fire to the stack, and the flame sprang up till it could be seen over the whole length and breadth of the Marsh. On Dundon Hill and Glastonbury Tor, on the distant hill by Wedmore, and on every side all around the Marsh the Easter fires then began to gleam like stars in the night. The black flag of Ragnar fell into the ashes on Athelney Mount. The heathen in Selwood and in the Mendip hills, seeing the fires, ran for their weapons. They said: 'It is the Marsh King's war signal!' But in the morning there was a bright and peaceful day, and they learned that the fires were only a custom of the people at this time of the year.

In the morning the King returned to Aller church with the bishop and Ethelnoth, and as many of the captains and men of the King's force as the boats could carry. There they celebrated Easter and received the Sacrament. Then, after Mass, the bishop placed the King's flag, the dragon of Wessex, upon the altar and consecrated it. The King took the flag and went again over the water at high tide to the Mount, and set it up there on the summit, and so it remained every day while the King was in the islands.

Four days after Easter Jarl Einar led a strong force through Shepton to Glastonbury, to burn and plunder. They met no opposition. There was nothing left to loot in Glastonbury. The monastery had been abandoned. Einar climbed the Tor and looked out over the Marsh, where only wild geese were seen, flying low over the boggy meres. There was no sign of men. He saw none anywhere on his march. The peasants had all fled from this region now, and the fields of the Selwood clearings were beginning to green over with weeds. Next day he returned to Froom going by way of Alham, which he found deserted round its roofless hall. Then, along the forest road, two miles beyond, they found men hanging by the neck from the trees. They were newly dead, all Danish men, and known to them.

In Froom Guthorm awaited him. He had come that morning, making a journey through his conquered territories. 'Where have you been, Einar?' said he. 'Have you been setting nets in the mud, to catch the Marsh King?'

'It will need more than a joke to deal with this matter,' replied Einar. 'A king ought to bring aid to his vassals when they are beset. We shall need strong help from your arm in this quarter, before we can hold it in peace. And where is this Saxon King Edgar you say is to do such wonders for us? It is time you brought him out from under your cloak.'

'I shall not jump too soon, and in the dark, like that fool Hubba,' said Guthorm, angrily. 'A fine day's work he did, going his own way without me, even without knowing his enemy. See what has come of it. When I know my enemy, then I shall know how to twist his neck. Who is he, this Marsh

King? What is his following? Am I to muster a whole army to catch some bandit in a bog? Find me these answers, Einar, and then I will do my part, whatever is needed.'

It was only the heathen at this time who did not know the answer. It was no secret in Selwood. In the forest villages, from this time onward King Alfred was seen often with his war-bands. In the regions south of Alham the enemy could not settle in peace, and north of it for a long way it was hazardous to try. Saxon churls and others in the north of Somerset who had thought it best to submit to Guthorm's rule were themselves not safe from punishment by the Saxon war-bands, or by their own neighbours. In a time of anarchy, neighbours will pay off old scores. Boundary stones were moved between farms, first in King Guthorm's name, then in King Alfred's. Jarl Einar came to hear of King Alfred, by name, before long, but he was not prepared to tell Guthorm before he had made sure. Jarl Torgils, he knew, had vowed that King Alfred was dead. 'That Torgils is a liar as well as a fool,' said Einar. There was no love lost between him and Torgils.

The buds were beginning to show on the trees. Selwood was full of primroses. In the fields the ploughmen and sowers were out. On his estate at Twyford, near Winchester, Ealdorman Wulfric and his reeve were talking of peas and beans when they saw two horsemen coming. They were King Alfred's messengers. When they had declared themselves, one opened his wallet and took out a piece of a loaf of bread, all burned as black as a cinder. This he handed to Wulfric. He said:

'The time and place are appointed. The second day of the second week of May, at King Egbert's stone.'

The same message was brought to Alfgar in Cranborne Chase, and to Edmund of Wiltshire, at Wilton. Thereupon all sent out the same sign to their own thanes, naming a time and place for the gathering of the shires.

CHAPTER THIRTY-THREE

A Guardian

THE LADY ELSWITHA with her family and household now left Winchester and came to Sherborne, to the King's vill. King Alfred went there from Athelney to greet her. With her came also many of the King's guard, whom he had left at Winchester to defend his household. Among these was the thane Escwin. They brought certain chests of treasure which the King had at Winchester, and from these he now gave gifts to his followers, swords and arm-rings and other things of great worth.

Alfgar was there with Elric, Waltruda's son. Elric had grown taller and looked almost a man. The King said to him: 'Alfgar has given me a good report of you, and I am willing that you should serve in my company.' The King gave him a baldrick with a gold buckle, for his sword. Elric was proud to take it. Then said the King:

'Go and find your sister Hildis and bring her here. I wish her to come to this household, serving the Lady Elswitha.'

Elric, therefore, went the following day to the convent at Donhead, where Hildis was. Elred his brother went with him. They saw their young sister again, and their mother, with great joy, for they had not known the Lady Waltruda was there.

Elric told Hildis of the King's wish, and that the Bishop of Sherborne also had allowed that she should go from the convent. Yet Hildis, though she was glad of this, did not wish once again to be parted from her mother. But Waltruda said:

'Go, child. This place is more suited to me than to you. I shall stay here, where at need you may always find me.'

Later that day Waltruda asked for Howel the serf to be sent

to her. He came from the farm and found her standing near the gate of the convent enclosure, within which were the chapel and the houses of the nuns.

She said to him:

'The time has come now for you to take your freedom. There is no more service you can do for me. I shall stay here, doing whatever I may to serve God. I, being myself a servant shall need no one to serve me.'

'Mistress,' said Howel, 'let me only stay here as a labourer on the farm. I am a serf. Whatever I have done in my life has been done in serfdom, for my master. I have not myself been responsible. But if I am free, my deeds are the deeds of my own hand. If my hand does evil, if it should kill, say if perhaps it might kill some young man at the beginning of his life, this would then be my own deed. Let me remain a serf, mistress. It would be better for me.'

Waltruda said: 'No, Howel, you are free. I refuse your serfdom. But if you will take service as a free man, there is a young man at the beginning of his life, such as you describe, whose life you may guard and keep. My son Elric is in his seventeenth year. He goes now with the King, to fight the King's battles. Go with him. Being free, you may carry arms and stand at his side in the shield-wall. Guard well this young man at the beginning of his life.'

Howel stood in silence for a long while. Then he said:

'I will do as you bid me, Lady Waltruda. I take my freedom now, for what it is worth. My sins be upon my own head.'

He turned and went and found Elric, Unferth's son. He went with him as a free man to King Alfred's stronghold in the marshes.

Hildis remained with the Lady Elswitha's household at Sherborne Vill, Waltruda at the convent of Saint Cuthberga. The Abbess allowed Waltruda a place there. She spent her time in work and prayer. The weather grew warm, the trees became pale with young leaves. Watching from the convent gate

Waltruda could see every day across the river, on the road going towards Shaftesbury, the armed men of the Dorset levies going to the gathering under Alfgar's war-banner.

CHAPTER THIRTY-FOUR

The Grinners

GUTHORM learned that King Osketil, his old rival, had died suddenly in East Anglia. This on the whole pleased him, though he was disturbed by a rumour that Osketil had died of poison. He began to ask himself how far his own chieftains were to be trusted. However, there was still the ever-threatening danger from the marshes of Somerset to keep them united under his leadership. The Marsh King had his uses, therefore, whoever he was.

But whoever he was, now that spring was here he was a challenger whom Guthorm knew he would have to meet. Yet, on the other hand, why should he, Guthorm, be led off into the bogs of Somerset to fight with a local headman whom the Saxons might later deal with on their own? Einar was right, he thought. The time had come to rig up the young Atheling Edgar, and push him into position on the throne of West Wessex, with a gang of newly-empowered thanes to manage his affairs for him under Guthorm's eye, for as long as Guthorm pleased. Let them settle the business of the Marsh King among themselves. Until they did, he was welcome to his marsh.

Edgar had spent three months in wretchedness at the black home of Agg the Sightless. There with his pale wife he waited for Guthorm to send for him. He avoided the blind man whenever he could, but by some sense the old man seemed to feel his presence whenever he was near.

'Are you here still, King of Wessex?' the old man would now say. 'I hear that my daughter's gown is ready, to come to your crowning.'

Guthorm sent Skafti Olafsson to bring Edgar to Chippenham. Edgar, though he was glad enough to be gone from Agg's house, was anxious about the reason for it. He feared Guthorm. His wife's brother Beorn went with him. They entered Guthorm's dwelling in Chippenham church, which was now very unclean. It was crowded. At the far end the three wooden gods that Guthorm had set up stood in a row on the altar, with King Alfred's cloak lying before them as usual. Guthorm sat on his throne nearby, playing at checkers with Olaf the Skald. When he saw Edgar he ended the game by kicking the board away, and rose to meet him with a grin which showed the gaps in his teeth. He behaved in a friendly manner and called Edgar 'brother'. He picked up the stool which the checker board had stood on, and set it for Edgar to sit down. But Beorn said bluntly:

'Must the King of Wessex sit on a stool, while Guthorm sits proudly on a throne?'

Guthorm was in a clownish mood. He made a great display of fetching two more stools, one for himself, one for Beorn. He carefully blew the dirt from the stool he offered Beorn, and wiped it with his sleeve. The buffoonery had a cold edge to it, however. When they were all seated he sent the rest of his people to stand further off, so that he could talk in private. He began to outline his plan, though it was vague, even in outline. He said he had sent for all his most important chieftains to help advise him on this matter. Many were already present, and others, including the Jarls Torgils and Einar, arrived while Guthorm was still talking. With their entry the subject of Edgar's claim to the throne of Wessex, and how it could be put into effect, was set aside for the moment. But it was a moment that did not pass. Never again, as it happened, was the subject taken up.

Torgils was in a passion. He had come face to face with Einar in the road outside Guthorm's hall, and had there at once opened upon a standing quarrel they had. There was a village under the steep side of the Wiltshire Downs, on the north-west corner, a place called Bratton. Above this village is the great and curious image of the horse, cut in the chalk on the hillside. The white beast on the hill can be seen for miles around. Perhaps it was the vanity of possessing this landmark, or perhaps it was for the sake of the old ramparts defending the hilltop above it, that both Torgils and Einar laid claim to the village, which was upon the boundary that Guthorm had drawn between their territories. After much dispute they had agreed to have Guthorm decide the matter, and had come here now more for this purpose than for any other. Torgils came in, limping, for his old leg-wound was aching, which did not help his temper.

'King Guthorm,' said he, 'I claim blood-payment from Einar here, for two of my people whom his men have killed outside Bratton village. They were upon my own land, defending themselves. I demand justice.'

Einar calmly said: 'The village is not yours, Torgils, and if any of your men were slain there it was not by the hand of any of mine. Therefore, do not spit your bile at me.'

Guthorm sat himself in his throne and said: 'Peace between you while I am here. Torgils, how can you be sure it was by Danish hands that your men were killed? Einar has had some of his own men slain not long since, but this was done by the Saxons. The Marsh King's men can creep into your lands as well as into his.'

'If he cannot defend his people against a handful of bog-brigands, that is his business,' Torgils said; 'but my people were treacherously attacked by Einar's underlings, not by any Saxons, and I shall prove it.'

Einar made a gesture of rage and scorn. 'Hear him, ye gods!' he cried, turning towards the three who stood grinning their wooden grins on the altar. 'Hear what he will prove, the boaster! Hear his lies! A handful of bog-brigands, is that all you found, Torgils, when you went fishing in the Marsh? If it is true you found no more than that, then you must have been blind and deaf. Who is the Marsh King, Torgils? Do you not know?'

Torgils replied hotly: 'Do not try to turn the matter aside, Einar. Pay me the blood-price for my men, murdered by yours.'

But Guthorm interrupted.:

'Hold your peace, Torgils. What was it Einar said? The Marsh King, Einar. What do you know?'

'Ha! I know only what Torgils has known all along. He has been deceiving you, Guthorm. Did he not say King Alfred was dead? Did he not tell you how cleverly he trapped King Alfred and his companions in the woodland hall on Edgar's wedding night? Tell us again of the great fight you had there, Torgils! Tell us again how King Alfred was slain. Oho, beyond doubt he was slain! But tell us also how it is that the forest is now full of King Alfred's fighting men, with Alfred himself alive and in arms to lead them! Tell us that, too!'

Guthorm sprang to his feet, his eyes wide, his mouth open. Torgils cried:

'By the gods, Einar, you are mad! You shall answer for this!' He had his hand on his sword's hilt. The bright weapon was half drawn from its sheath. Guthorm angrily held his arm.

'Do you not answer him, Einar,' he ordered. 'Answer me! Is this true? Is Alfred living? How do you know it? Speak!'

Torgils pulled his arm free and shouted: 'Yes! Speak Einar. But prove your words. You shall rue this!'

'Rue it yourself, Torgils, liar! Every man knows it. Ask anywhere. Alfred is alive, and fighting. Who else is the Marsh King?'

Torgils stood back from him and from grim Guthorm. The heathen men in the hall were still. Torgils, standing upright, his head high, his fists clenched against his thighs, his voice shaking with anger, spoke in the silence:

'Odin, hear me. Guthorm, hear me. By the gods, Einar, hear me you also, and all who stand here! Who will dare to say again that I have lied? There are some here who were with me that night at the Dragon Hall. Stand forth, my companions! Did we not fight like heroes against heroes; did we not slay them all, one by one, shield to shield? And are we now to be called cowards and liars for our pains? Is this our reward? I tell you, Guthorm, and this is true, there was one man and one only who escaped our sharp swords and the blackening fire, and he was not Alfred, not he. Believe it!'

Einar cried out: 'Ha! So you admit it! One man!'

'I will kill you, Einar!' Torgils shouted in reply. 'You shall not live!'

'Hold your peace, both!' Guthorm said, sharply. He stood between them. 'By my blood, if Alfred is alive still and in the field, what can it matter now how it came about? But it matters greatly that he should not come upon us and find us fighting among ourselves. Peace, therefore. I command it!'

But peace had no place there. It was now broken from another quarter. There was a sudden stir at the hall door, and Jarl Sigurd Hammerfist came hastening in, muddy from hard riding.

'You bade me come, King Guthorm,' said he, breaking in. He took no heed of the anger he found there. 'By the hammer of Thor,' he said 'I should have come in any case, bidden or not. Have you heard nothing, Guthorm, that your men are not in arms? I tell you there is warfare brewing!'

'Ha! Warfare within and without,' Guthorm said. 'What is it with you, Sigurd?'

'The Saxons are in the field,' Jarl Sigurd said. 'They are mustering everywhere. They are marching towards the downland and the plain. It means battle, beyond any doubt. They say King Alfred himself has sent out the war signal.'

'So it is King Alfred? You have heard that?' Guthorm said.

'Heard it? It is heard like a trumpet. I am taking no risks. I have summoned in my men from their newly-gotten lands, and we are marching to join you. The Christians are going to make a fight of it after all, and with Alfred leading them it will be hard.'

'Hear that, Torgils, Alfred-Slayer!' mocked Einar.

'Curb your tongue, Einar!' Guthorm commanded. 'This is not a time for it. Go, sound the war-horn in Selwood, call in your men to form their war-bands. Out, all! But Torgils, stay you here.

The warriors crowded noisily from the hall. There was a clamour of shouting, of horses, there was a trumpet blown. Einar went wrathfully out. Wrathfully Torgils stood where he was.

'Why must I wait, King Guthorm?' he demanded. 'Do not venture to curse at me. I have deserved better of you. Here, take back your gifts.' He pulled off the gold arm-rings he was wearing and would have flung them on the ground before Guthorm, but Guthorm stayed him.

'Keep them, Torgils. I did not bid you stay for that reason. I would not have had you and Einar go out together, to cut each other's throats in the road, that was all. As for King Alfred, if it is indeed true that he is still alive, there can only be one reason for that. It is his luck, his luck, Torgils! The luck of Wessex has saved him yet once again. Therefore, how can you be blamed? By the gods, but his luck cannot last for ever. Go, Torgils; let us all make ready for the battle. This time, at last, we shall see an end to it all!'

So Torgils went out, keeping Guthorm's gifts. Evening crept into the house, filling it with shadows. Guthorm thought himself alone. He did not see Olaf and his son Skafti standing in a dark corner by the far door. He went slowly towards the altar where the three gods stood, grinning, as ever, with their carved mouths and their wooden eyes. Dim they were in the shadows, but Guthorm could see them grinning.

'Grin, then, grin!' he cried out suddenly. He held his hands with clenched fists above his head. 'Fine work you have done for me, you grinners!' He was shouting at them. His voice was choked and stumbling in his rage. 'From Jutland I have brought you, all the way, tenderly, with care. You were like my parents to me, you were like my children. You have had the best work of my blood and hands. Have I not kept every vow I made you? But what have you done for me? Do you not stand upon Christian altars as I promised? Yet what have you done to earn it? What luck have you brought me? What luck have you brought even to yourselves? You have let the Christian god pull the wool over your eyes. You have let him make fools of you, as you have made a fool of me. Grin away, then, grin!' he cried. 'Blockheads!' And suddenly he rushed at them, flinging out his arms wildly, and the three wooden gods tumbled woodenly to the dirty floor.

Guthorm leaned his back against the altar table for a moment. He was breathing heavily. Then he went and picked up the gods one by one, and pitched them into the corner beside the altar, one on top of the other, as if they were nothing but logs for the fire.

'Lie there, then, and grin for as long as you please,' he said. 'Stay there until you have learned how to do better for the friends who have trusted you. As for me, we shall see whether I cannot do better on my own.'

He then bent down and picked up King Alfred's red cloak which had fallen with the gods from the altar to the ground. He held it at arm's length and looked at it a moment in the dimness of the hall, by the last faint light of evening which came in through the great door at the end. Towards this door Guthorm suddenly threw the cloak, with all his strength. Then he ran down the hall and jumped on the cloak with both feet. It was a ridiculous action. He picked it up and tried to tear it, but it was too tough at the hem, he could not start it. He was panting with rage. He drew his knife and hacked at the hem. Then dropping the knife and standing on one part of the cloak he pulled at the other until it began to rend in two. He tugged, breathing hard, till it all parted at last at the collar. Then he began to tug and tear at each piece. 'Alfred!' he shouted, 'Alfred!' He tore at the pieces. 'You with your luck!' He tore the pieces, panting. 'We shall see, we shall see!' When he had finished tearing he picked up all the pieces in a bundle and flung them from him as far as he could. 'Come on then, Alfred! I shall be ready for you. See what good your luck will do for you now. Come on to the battlefield at last!'

Then Guthorm stood awhile in silence, his chin upon his chest, his hands hanging at his side. He grew calm. He raised his head and walked slowly towards the open door. He went out. He had not seen the watchers in the shadows.

Outside it was nearly dark. In the far forest under the evening star a hollow horn-call sounded and the note faded sadly away. The night came.

CHAPTER THIRTY-FIVE

At Egbert's Stone

AT the highest point on the wide plain of Wiltshire, seven miles east of Selwood, at a place where many trackways meet coming together from every part of Wessex, stands King Egbert's Stone. It is a landmark seen for miles around, a solitary finger upon a treeless skyline. Here, years ago, returning from the conquest of the Cornish Welsh, King Egbert had halted his army. Here his shire levies had parted, each upon his own homeward road. First, however, to commemorate their victory, they had set up this great stone. Carved upon it were the words EGBERT OF WESSEX KING VICTORIOUS STOOD ME HERE. Now to this same place the armies of Wessex were coming back, grandsons of Egbert's soldiers answering his grandson Alfred's call, at the appointed time. From Hampshire under Wulfric's banner came one thousand five hundred men. From Wiltshire came a thousand. These marched in small parties at first, to avoid attracting the attention of the enemy. Alfgar waited at Shaftesbury with a thousand men of Dorset. All were encamped in wooded valleys a few miles from the trysting-place, waiting for the day. They lay in green meadows and plucked the new leaves above them, and talked with neighbours from nearby villages who in a busy life they rarely saw. They mingled for the first time with villagers from distant shires which for the most of them were nothing but a name. So passed warm and idle days, while only a few miles away on the empty plain the great grey stone stood alone, awaiting them.

In the late afternoon of the first day of the second week in May a party of horsemen from the heathen army, sent to spy upon the Saxons, ventured out onto the Plain from the north, and rode to within a short distance of the stone. They saw a party of men nearby, and saw that they were all armed. The leader of the Danish party, a young man whose name was Finn, reined in his horse and counted the number of Saxons. There were about thirty of them. At the approach of the Danes they had grouped themselves together, as if ready to fight. But Finn, having only half their number, would not venture on it. He turned and rode away as fast as he could with his men. He went back to the heathen outpost on the northern edge of the Plain, twelve miles away. 'We will watch that place again in the morning,' said he.

That night, at last, all the Saxon companies marched up from the meadows onto the Plain. Their leaders went back and forth on horseback from company to company, keeping them together on the night march to the steep hillside. King Egbert's Stone waited for them, a gaunt sentry on the Plain. Company by company the armed men drew near. All around within sight of the Stone they made their camp for the night, three thousand and five hundred men.

That same night the King's stronghold of Athelney stood empty. The King's men were marching eastward. Shortly before the sun went down over the Marsh, Escwin and Bracwealla climbed to the top of the Mount and took down the great flag which had stood there ever since Easter. They brought it to the King below, who was waiting armed in his boat. Then the oarsmen pulled away and rowed upstream to Langport. One hundred mounted men waited there for the King. When the boat came to the shore and the King stepped on land he knelt down, and Bishop Athelheah in armour, blessed him and besought God's blessing upon the great enterprise which was now beginning.

So the King mounted his horse. Escwin on his left carried the Dragon Flag of Wessex. On his right was the lord bishop's flag-bearer with the banner of Christ's Cross. Guntram the Frank rode next behind the King, wearing his great hauberk of iron plates and his huge helmet. With him went Bracwealla the armour-bearer, and Cnebba the King's body thane. Alfred the Dane-Leg, the secretary, rode with them also, young as he was, and without armour, riding among the stark and great men, among the coats of horn and iron. All the hundred of the King's men waited, ready and mounted in a body. Their horses snorted with impatience.

The King's trumpeter was named Hothric. He had a trumpet of white ivory, made of the whole tusk of an elephant, mounted with gold. It was a great treasure. It was said to have belonged to King Clovis in ancient times, and to have sounded for battle when Clovis overthrew Alaric the Goth. It had belonged in Hothric's family for three hundred years. He kept it wrapped in a sheepskin, hidden in his house. He called it Sky-Ringer. Hothric now rode his horse up onto a bank at the side of the road where all could see him, and he unwrapped Sky-Ringer from the sheepskin, and held it over his head gleaming in the setting sun, for all to see. Then King Alfred gave him the sign. Hothric put Sky-Ringer to his lips and blew. Like the noise of the great elephant its father trumpeting in the burning forests of the south went the note of Sky-Ringer, out over marsh and hill, into the west, into the east, into the purple sky. The men shouted and the King spurred his horse and led them forward. Thus it began.

Soon after nightfall, while the white dust of the road could still be seen in the dark, the King came to Cadbury Hill. Here Ethelnoth awaited him with the army of the Somerset men. The others of the King's men from Athelney were there also, having marched earlier in the day. In all there were one thousand and five hundred men.

Lying on the hillside among the King's men was young Elric of Alham, wrapped in his cloak. Nearby sat Howel who served and guarded him. Other men from Alham were there also, Prayn who had once been reeve, and Penda once falconer of the vill, once Duri's father. Rotri the smith was there also,

his harp held in the crook of his arm. As he gently touched the strings, making a magic sound in the night, he saw at a distance the torches and the stir of the King's arrival.

Rotri sang of the King's coming: *Now stand the soldiers, now the King's tent is lit with lamps. Now Alfred comes to his camp-fire, Ethelwulf's son, courageous in battle. The King has come to his war-host, and the heart of the kingdom beats boldly with valiant blood.*

Ethelnoth had set up his tent in the midst of the army, and here the King slept that night for three hours. Thereafter he rose to say his prayers and to read in his book. The soldiers watched his shadow in the lamplight on the walls of his tent. Long before dawn he was armed and ready for the day's march. All over the hillside the soldiers were stamping out their fires, gathering into companies, their war-gear ready. The May morning mists floated in long webs from the stream below, and the companies moved down to the trodden road, stirring the mist-webs as they went. Sky-Ringer sounded his note outside the King's tent at dawn, and when the sun rose he found the army already on the road, the King himself leading, going now towards the Plain, to the meeting-place at Egbert's Stone.

And in the grey waking of that same morning Finn the heathen was also in his saddle, out with his men over the wide bare Plain, riding towards the Stone. They rode in light mist as through a melting smoke. 'Come, sunrise', said Finn, 'or we shall lose our way.' 'Hush!' said another. They halted, listened. They heard horses and men's voices ahead of them in the mist, at some distance. 'Come, sunrise,' Finn whispered, listening. The mist warmed, grew light, began to melt. The red sun glowed through it. 'We have come too far,' said Finn. Through the opening mist half a mile away stood the grey Stone. All around it the green downland was blackened and crowded with men. As the mist widened away it revealed more and more the wide spread of the thousands of Wessex encamped on the hill. The sun began to glitter upon them. 'Back, then!' cried Finn. 'By the Old Three, now, we have our answer! Back!' They turned and rode fast trying to catch and hide in the last webs of mist. But the Saxons had seen them. There came a number on horseback, riding after them; but they could not be caught. Then one of the Saxons, a Hampshire man named Eafa, dismounted from his horse and put an arrow to his bow and drew it right to the head. He was a famous bowman. He let the arrow fly and it came down like lightning upon one of the Danes named Hjalti, striking him between the shoulders so that he fell dead at once upon the neck of his horse as he galloped. By some chance he did not fall, and his companions saw him riding there, dead. 'He is riding to Valhalla,' said they. So they outrode the Saxons and came to the northward roadway, and here they took Hjalti's horse, and left him there at the roadside propped against a stone with his eyes open and the arrow in his back; for they had no time to bury him. They rode like the wind to the heathen outpost and sent word to Guthorm.

King Alfred and the Somerset men marched eastward all that morning through the fair trees of Selwood along the ancient road called the Hardway, the same way that King Egbert had marched from Cornwall, and they came presently to the steep ascent of the Great Down. At the top of the hill as they approached it they saw a crowd of people waiting. They were poor country people who had left their fields and cottages to see the King as he passed. From the top of that hill the view is wide, far out over the valley. The army could be seen a mile away, the fluttering of its flags and cloaks, the shine on the shield-faces coming among the trees. The advance party now ascended to the crest of the hill, urging their horses up, and they cleared a way through the waiting country-folk. The King's banners came soon after, and after that the King himself. Then came the bishop and the ealdorman, the man with the white trumpet, the men in hauberks of iron. Here, then, at the hilltop the King called a halt, and the army rested. Company after company as they came up lay down on the hilltop, and the trees around them were all hung with their shields, an orchard of warlike fruit. At the crest of the hill there had once stood a great oak-tree. This had fallen, stricken with age and lightning, but its roots and stump still remained, like a great throne on the hilltop, cushioned with moss. Here, then, with a cloak spread for him, King Alfred sat for this short while on his march. The place to this day is called King's Seat Hill.

Some villagers had brought a water cart from their well, and were going around among the soldiers, giving them to drink. One of these came to the King. The King as he took the cup at once knew the man, and the woman who was with him, holding a baby. There was also a little boy. The King asked the man: 'Do you live far from here?'

'Not far, lord,' the man answered. 'A short distance down below the hill, by Penselwood yonder.'

'Is there not an old woman, your wife's mother, who lives in your house?' asked the King. 'Is all well with her?'

The man stared at the King, astonished. He answered: 'All is well enough, lord, but she is rather stiff in the joints, poor thing. You know how old she is.'

'I only know that she is old.' said the King. 'But I know also that the baby yonder was born at the New Year when there was snow on the ground, and at the time when you found a sick man sheltering in your straw.'

'Why, lord, that is true,' said the man. He smiled, pleased that this was known to the King.

The King said: 'Do you not know me?'

The man answered: 'Lord King, I am a poor man. How should I know you, being what I am.'

'Yet I know you, as you see,' said the King.

'Ah, yes, lord, but that is natural, since you are the King,' said the man. 'It is the King's task to know his people, so they say. Now I see it is true.'

King Alfred answered: 'The King is a man like other men. It was I myself who was your guest that night.'

The man said: 'Lord King, whatever you tell me I will certainly believe.'

Bishop Athelheah, who was standing by, said: 'That was well answered. Surely, my lord, the man's faith and loyalty are very touching.'

'Indeed they are,' said the King, 'but also, they are based upon the truth. The odd thing is, it seems this is what may never be believed.'

The bishop then blessed the man and his family, who went happily away, and, soon after, the King rose to his feet, and the army continued its march. They left the trees behind. They entered the wide Plain. Egbert's Stone stood upon the distant horizon.

Back to the army at the Stone the outpost men galloped. They were shouting: 'The King! The King is coming!' The trumpets answered their shout, trumpets of Dorset, of Wiltshire, of Hampshire, trumpets of horn and brass and bronze. The men of the shires under their banners saw the King coming in the distance. Sky-Ringer from the distance answered the brass and the bronze, the voice of the elephant tusk bellowed. The King rode out ahead of his men, the wide plain was filled with the galloping of the King's horse-guard. Then as the King drew near, the men of Egbert's Stone ran out to greet him. In long avenues they ranged themselves on each side, beating their shields and shouting 'Alfred! Alfred! King!' The King rode this way and that turning among them, their spears and banners waving around him almost hiding him in the tumult of their welcome. The great ealdormen opened a way at last with their thane-guards, for the King to come through to them at the foot of the Stone, and the thousands of Wessex gathered in a great circle around, still shouting 'Alfred! Alfred! King!' Never in Wessex had any king known such a welcome.

For one night more the army lay camped at Egbert's Stone.

Here with his chieftains the King made his plan for the next day's march, and for the battle, whenever that might be. He knew well what he intended.

At dawn, then, the army marched, troop after troop, going northward. They marched spread out over the plain. Presently, in the centre, those of the vanguard stopped and pointed. They had come upon the body of the Dane, Hjalti. There he lay, propped against his stone, his eyes open, with the arrow in his back, the point showing through his chest. The Saxons were cheered to see him. 'So be it with them all,' said they. Eafa the marksman said: 'That was my arrow.' The army marched past on either side, and presently there was nothing left in sight on the wide plain but only the dead man seeing nothing, and the great Stone lonely on the skyline. The sky-larks sang high overhead on the empty morning air.

But now, miles to the north that same morning, in the heathen camp at Chippenham, all Guthorm's war-horns were sounding, so that the black rooks flew from the trees in terror. Guthorm laughed to see them flapping out. His men like the rooks in their thousands were ready, their spear-beaks eager for blood. For this day Guthorm had long waited. Now the jarls of his savage army led out their men, all greedy for the blood-red battlefield, laughing and whistling as they marched southward. Before they left their camp they sacrificed a horse to Odin their one-eyed god, black as Satan. A black horse they chose for sacrifice. They slit its neck-vein and drove it ahead of them till it dropped. It went a great distance. This they considered a good omen.

CHAPTER THIRTY-SIX

Armies Approaching

THE land at the north-west corner of the Plain is like a table with a cleft in it. The cleft is the valley of the River Wylye. This runs out towards the north-west, cutting the Plain just below the corner, so that the corner stands up like a tongue of high land between north and south. This part of the Plain is called Ethandune. To the south of it, in the river valley, is Iley Wood. To the north, in the shadow of the steep hillside is the vill of Bratton. On the high plain of Ethandune that lies between, guarding the steep sides of it, overlooking the valleys below, there are many banks and ditches of ancient strongholds. None can remember who dug them there. The hawks are lonely that hover above them. Even the White Horse cut there in the hillside has long forgotten the people who dug those old earthworks upon his back.

Guthorm the Dane marched his great army southward to the fields of Bratton under Ethandune hill. He sent out scouting parties on horseback. Some went up the steep hill onto the plain, others went round below under the White Horse till they came near the Wylye valley; but here they met with the advance parties of the Saxons, and they quickly withdrew. On the hill above it, was the same; on the open Plain the advance parties of the Saxons and the heathen saw each other at a distance and halted. They stood watching each other for a while, breathing their horses, neither side willing to leave the field to the other; but after a while, without even a word shouted between them, both parties suddenly turned and galloped away, back to their armies, neither side knowing which had made the first move.

Guthorm called his war-council. He sat with his sword Fang

across his knees, the blade bare, the edge newly keen from the grindstone. All his fierce jarls and chieftains were there, the whole pack. Torgils and Einar watched each other from opposite sides of the circle. They hated each other more than they hated Saxons. Sigurd Hammerfist sat in the midst. He eyed King Guthorm sharply, thinking himself the better man. Guthorm spoke:

'Now, chieftains, now at last you are in sight of your greatest conquest. It is I, Guthorm, who have brought it to you. I have dragged out the Christians from their Wessex bogs, from their woods and hiding-holes. I have brought them to you on the battlefield, which for seven long years they have avoided. They lie there just over the hill in the river valley. Tonight we shall go up onto the Plain and wait for them. They will come, they cannot avoid it. That will be the end of them, and the end of King Alfred. Strike, strike at Alfred! Make an end of him! The days of his luck are over! Make an end of him, and all Wessex is ours!'

Guthorm struck his sword into the ground again and again, shouting: 'An end of Alfred! Bring me his head! Wessex is ours!' The jarls applauded him. It was a tone they liked to hear. Nevertheless Sigurd thought that Guthorm's heart was less confident than his words.

King Alfred's army was camped in Iley Wood. His watchers stood on the hilltop above, looking out over empty Ethandune in the evening, while the King held his war-council. The ealdormen and thanes sat silently in a half-circle on the ground while the King stood before them and spoke:

'Lords of Wessex, the enemy lies yonder just over the hill. Tomorrow comes the battle. You know how many battles we have fought against this same enemy, this ignorant enemy of God, this thief and spoiler of the harvests of mankind. Some battles we have won, as at Ashdown; some we have lost, as at Marten, where the King my brother took his death-wound. We have dared all battles, win or lose. But tomorrow for the first time we may say we dare not, for tomorrow is the battle we dare not lose. Win tomorrow, lords, and all is won. Lose and all is lost. Now at last it is all or nothing. We dare not lose.'

So the King and the lords of Wessex made up their battle-order, and then the lords went back to the camping-places of their own shire-levies, and the King sat for a while in his tent, dictating letters to his secretary, young Alfred the Dane-Leg. When all this was done he said:

'Now, Namesake, tomorrow's battle cannot be for you, as you know. You must saddle up and leave at once. Go back and wait for me at Sherborne. If it is God's will that I come alive out of the battle we shall have much work together in the future, more than we have ever done before. But if I do not come back, then the memory of whatever I have tried to do in this kingdom may rest in your hands, and those of the few others who, like yourself, I have had trained in writing. Alas, too few. You cannot be spared or risked. Go now, and remember what I have told you.'

So the secretary sadly left the King, as he was commanded, and rode away through the camp with certain others of the King's servants. As they went, all the camp was full of restless preparation. The lords of the shires had brought their priests with them, and these had set up altar-tables, with torches burning by them to mark where they were, and all night long they said Mass and the soldiers came and knelt and received the holy bread and wine, the gift of God, and thus fortified returned to make ready for the day. Few there were so hardy they could sleep that night, but all sat wrapped in their cloaks watching the coming and going in the camp, talking little. Elric of Alham sat silent listening to Rotri the smith, who was singing softly to his harp. Elric trembled within himself, not from fear but from the brilliance of excitement. The man Howel sat near, watching.

Between the first and the second hour of morning the word came from Ethelnoth to the Somerset men to make ready; so they stood with their weapons, and presently Ethelnoth began to lead them out of Iley Wood and up the hill towards Ethandune. The path went up between two old earth-works crowning two spurs of the hill, about a mile apart. Here strong outposts of the Wessex army had been stationed, and these now looked down on the long dark movement of the Somerset army climbing the hill between them. A mile ahead of them the path went up steeply to the crest of the Down, where there was an ancient ditch banked up on the far side, to defend the hilltop. Before reaching this the main body of the Somerset men were halted, while Ethelnoth and his thane-guard went ahead alone, cautiously approaching the summit. As they reached the ditch, those waiting below heard sudden cries and shouts, like the sharp snarling of animals finding enemies in the night. A strong advance party of the heathen were already there, having lain hidden in the ditch, waiting for reinforcements. These indeed were not far away, coming along just beyond the crest of the hill. Ethelnoth had reached the place only just in time. He shouted from the hilltop, and the rest of the Somerset men began to climb up. It was still too dark for fighting, however. None could tell friend from foe. But even by starlight the heathen could tell they were outnumbered. They left the ditch and began to run back along this hill, warning the others. One of Ethelnoth's thanes, the first to find the enemy in the ditch, was killed, but there was no other hurt, and Ethelnoth held the hilltop.

Soon after, the main body of the Wessex army began to leave the wood and march up the hill towards Ethandune. Now, with Guntram the Frank and two of his thanes, and two grooms who were later to take back the horses, the King rode past the marching men to this hilltop where Ethelnoth awaited him. On a knoll midway up the hill the bishop of Sherborne stood with the priests. They carried with them holy relics of Saint Boniface and Saint Aldhelm, which were known to have miraculous powers, and these they held out over the soldiers as they went past, over the iron-black war helmets, over the moving hedges of barbed spears. Thus all the army was blessed as it marched up to Ethandune. First after the King came the lord Edmund with the Wiltshire men. Then Alfgar of Dorset; and lastly the Hampshire men, led by Ealdorman Wulfric, carrying the banner of his shire which his wife and her women had woven and embroidered for him with the device of a stag's head.

Now the King led the whole army forward onto the Plain of Ethandune, under stars that were beginning to pale with the coming of dawn. He halted at a position facing north looking along the saddle of the Down. Here it was about half a mile wide. On each side it dropped away steeply. In front, however, the Down spread out wider, so that the enemy, too, could spread as wide on each flank as he chose; but with the Saxons standing on the narrower part, to come upon their flank the heathen would have to descend a small valley and come at them again uphill. Here then the Saxons stood, drawing their battle line across the Down, Ethelnoth on the left, then Alfgar, then Edmund, then Wulfric on the right. As the darkness bleached itself to grey they suddenly hushed and listened, for away in the distance ahead they could hear the noises of an approaching mob, a strange murmuring noise, pierced with yelps like hunting dogs, with horn-calls and shouts, and with a sound of laughter. It came nearer and nearer. The Saxons were silent. One heard from them only the sound of their banners and pennants flapping in the dawn wind. Then came the drumming of horses' hoofs galloping on the turf, as the King with Guntram at his side, with Escwin and Bracwealla carrying the great banners of Wessex, with the bishop also, in his armour, with the ealdormen and the banner-bearers of the shires, galloped along the whole length of the line, showing the banners to the army in the growing light. The cheering of the men and the blowing of horns then followed them along the whole army. From the approaching heathen an answering clamour of horns broke out. Each answered each, and a stridor of terrible trumpeting curdled the morning sky over Ethandune. The great lords galloped back to their places, the King returned with his banners to the centre. He dismounted among the warriors. The horses were sent away. The huge army of the pagans, bellowing like cattle, yelping like dogs, clattering with armour of horn and iron and bronze, bristling with spears and emblems of skulls and antlers and wings of birds, came towards them in a long, howling line stretching right across the Down. Blacker and greater they grew as they approached. Then at last they halted a hundred yards away, still leaping and shouting in their shaggy ranks, rattling and brandishing their weapons. The Saxons were silent. Grimly they stood in the long shield-wall and waited.

CHAPTER THIRTY-SEVEN

Ethandune

GRIMLY rode Guthorm to the front of the heathen battle-line. Loudly the howls of the heathen acclaimed him, their horn-men blew the bellowing war-horns. Guthorm rode with his chieftains part way towards the Saxon shield-wall, and he shouted:

'Alfred the Saxon. Alfred the Skulker! Where are you? Come out, come out and show yourself!'

Alfred the King answered:

'I am here, Guthorm. You see me.' He stepped forward from the centre of the Saxon line. Bracwealla went with him on his right hand, Guntram on his left. They held their shields ready.

'I see you, King Skulker,' Guthorm taunted, 'and I hear you also. I have heard you before, I have heard you too often. You once said you would teach me something if I came to you again. I have come, Alfred, but now it is I who will do the teaching.'

'Begin, then,' answered Alfred the King. 'We here are waiting for you.'

But Guthorm shouted: 'Let the learner come to the teacher. Come out, Skulker Alfred, come and get your lesson.'

'You are in my land,' replied Alfred. 'You have travelled a long way to find me. Now you see me. You have only a few more paces to go, Guthorm. Are you afraid to take the step?'

Then the whole Saxon battle-line laughed and taunted: 'Come on, Guthorm! Are you afraid?'

The heathen army shouted in reply and began to come further forward; but the Christians stood where they were under their banners, a steady wall. Guthorm in a rage reined his horse about and rode returning to his ranks. He and his leaders sent back their horses and stood on foot ready for battle. Then Einar shouted mockingly to Jarl Torgils, along the line:

'There he stands, Torgils Alfred-Slayer, there he stands! Fine work, hero! Show us today how it is done!'

'Better you die in battle, Einar,' Torgils shouted back to him 'for you shall not escape me afterwards! Ravens shall eat you! You shall have no burial, I vow it!'

'Fools!' Guthorm shouted to them in his turn. 'There stands your enemy yonder. Is this a place to quarrel among yourselves? Go forward!'

So the jarls led the pagan line farther forward. They came on now step by step, crouching and wary, drumming with their weapons on their shields, beating in time together, and shouting together in time with the shield-beat: 'Dog, dog, dog! Kill, kill, kill!' Not far now from the Saxon host, the heathen halted once more. On the far flanks their long line came to the downward slopes of the hill. They began to draw towards the middle to avoid descending below the Saxon line. They stood together shouting: 'Kill, kill, kill!'

Guntram the Frank at King Alfred's side said:

'The blood beats in me, Lord King! By the Cross, there is something about this day! It is success. I know the feeling ahead of time. It sings in the blood. King, you cannot fail!'

Alfred looked around to him. 'You also, Guntram, you have this! You are right: it sings in the blood, in mine also! Ha! Though this should be my last battle, I tell you it is the first I have ever felt as I feel now. This time we cannot fail. It sings in the air!'

Hothric the trumpeter stood by him. Sky-Ringer gleamed in his hands. He looked at the King, making ready to put the gold mouthpiece to his lips. But the King said: 'Not yet. Let them come first to their teacher.'

In the heathen battle-rank Olaf the Skald sang loud above the beating and baying of the host. He chanted a hero-song to stir the hot blood. He sang:

> The spear-wave shall rage in the hero's storm,
> Under the iron-trimmed shield the blood-waves shall roar in Odin's gale,
> Though many a warrior sinks under the stream of swords
> They shall ride Valhalla's red road to the hero's feasting.

This and much like it sang Olaf in the tumult of shouting, but at his side he saw his young son Skafti standing with weapons in his first battle, and within him his heart sang: 'Ah, Skafti, my son, go back, leave all this and live for another season under the friendly sky!' But now there was no going back.

Once more Eafa the marksman drew an arrow to its head. The shaft flew, and struck its mark. Thus the first Dane fell dead. Then a great cloud of Saxon arrows shot forth like a storm of hail suddenly. The heathen shields shuddered with striking. Heathen arrows answered and the heathen host moved forward again crowding together on the level ground. Spears and arrows darted from the Saxon shield-wall till the gap between the armies was closed under the flashing sword-storm, shield against shield.

'Now, Wessex, now!' cried Alfred the King. 'Strike now for Christ's kingdom. Strike now for King Edmund, the arrow-martyr! Out, heathen, out! Guthorm, you have come to your master!'

Escwin the thane held the dragon-flag near to the King. Guthorm saw it and it guided him, but he could not come near, so strong was the shield-press. Sigurd Hammerfist beat the wall with his sword, but could not move it. The gashing spears beat him back. Edmund the ealdorman saw Sigurd, ravager

of Wiltshire, and pressed towards him, clearing a path with his swinging sword. Jarl Sigurd faced him. He cried: 'Back, boy!' Their swords like hammers rose and fell. Denwald, Edmund's thane, saw the ealdorman hard pressed. He ran towards him, he and others, but none could come at stark Sigurd, the sword-swinger. Denwald's shield was split, and he reeled back with the blow. The savage spears of the heathen caught him then, and he fell dying underfoot.

Then cried Guntram the Frank: 'Out, heathen!' He saw Edmund of Wiltshire struck down under Sigurd's heavy blows. He battered through the mob with his strong shield till he faced Sigurd, and with a great blow of his sword he sent the jarl staggering back, off his balance. The jarl's men closed round him till he picked himself up. Guthorm from a little distance laughed to see Sigurd on his knees. Yet he had little enough time for laughter. Ethelnoth came to the front of the battle, seeking his foe. He saw Guthorm and made towards him. Elric of Alham was in that part of the field also, with Howel at his side. The battle-storm burst all round them. Blood like rain ran dripping from the warriors' shields. Ethelnoth pinned in the press saw Guthorm no more. He shook himself free and strode striking in amongst the heathen, beating them back. He trod over bodies. He then stood facing Skafti the boy, he, Ethelnoth the grim warrior. Then cried Olaf, Skafti's father, 'Stand, Saxon!' He struck Ethelnoth a blow so that the ealdorman staggered. Then the battle shifted around them and they faced different foes. Skafti stood face to face with Elric of Alham in the midst of the red field. Skafti struck out at Elric with his spear, but the blow was taken on another shield. Howel thrust Skafti away with his spear butt, and dragged Elric back to the shield wall which had drawn together again after the loosening blows of the heathen onslaught.

Then the two sides stood for a moment apart, and saw the ground between heavy with dead men. But Alfred saw that the Saxon shield-wall was a steady line, the heathen host a mass of men unsteady of leadership, sure of their courage but unsure how to use it. Then he called:

'Now, Hothric, sound!'

Then Sky-Ringer bellowed out his elephant note over the armies, the Saxon war-horns down the long shield-wall sounded, the Christian host shouted with a great shout and the shield-wall advanced over the dead and dying men towards the foe. The heathen fell back before them. Young Elric pushed forward among the warriors, feeling the battle-thrill in his blood. Then from the heathen ranks, swinging an axe among iron-crusted hauberks, among helmets of brass and gold, seeing only eyes of anger and eyes of death, seeking only to slay, caring not whom, Jarl Torgils came. He swung the axe over Elric, but he brought it down upon the man Howel who ran between. He stood against the tide of the Saxon battle-line, trying to stem the flood with his axe, but he was pressed back as the flood pressed on. Howel lay dying on the ground and young Elric knelt over him. He called to him, 'Howel, Howel!' and Howel answered, calling faintly back from a great distance down the dark road of death, 'Ah, Duri!' The feet of the advancing Saxons went round them. Sky-Ringer bellowed on ahead.

Now stand the battle-banners in the midst of a heavy tide. They can move no way. The spear-forest is gripped in a grinding press. Death itself cannot die, so great is the crush of men; the dead cannot fall down. Yet slowly trampling, slowly grinding, slowly thrusting with hampered weapons the Saxons move forward till like the sudden breaking of ice after winter the heathen host parts in two halves, to the east and to the west, and the Saxon flood drives through at last.

Torgils stood axe in hand in the eastern part. His blood-red comrades shouted their defiant scorn at the Hampshire men, at the Wiltshire men, who, though now leaderless, drove at them with their savage spears. From Hampshire Wulfric stood forth. The thane Sithgar stood at his side. They saw

Torgils there with his axe. They went at him together. Little now can Torgils do. Little now can the heathen battle do on the downward hill. The Saxons cry: 'This for God and King Alfred! This for So-and-So!' They named friends long dead in many a battle. Torgils stood on the upper part of the slope. He saw his stark and savage comrades around him begin to go back, to give ground. He saw those conquerors of half the world beginning to run away. Yet still, sweating in the last sweat of his lifetime, Torgils stood, striking with his axe. 'This, then, for me!' he cried, swinging the axe. 'Go, life! Out, daylight!' Wulfric stood to him. Sithgar stood to him. 'Strength is strength!' cried Torgils, and his strength left him. They slew him where he stood.

The plain of Ethandune is filled now with running men, with the flight of arrows, the flinging of sharp spears. The heathen host runs back to right and to left, to east and to west. The hindmost must stop and defend themselves, forming their shield-walls in scattered companies all over the wide hill. Fierce battles are fought there. Yet the main heathen army, now in two parts, is driven back by the pursuing Saxons. King Guthorm himself cannot hold the line. He is forced back with the eastern half of his army, down the slope and into the valley that leads from high Ethandune to Bratton village below. Nothing can help him, fighting avails nothing, he must retreat with whatever part of his army he can save, to the fields below and the woods beyond. Wulfric and Ethelnoth and all the levies of Somerset, Wiltshire, and Hampshire are following close behind, hot for final victory.

On high Ethandune hill, the jarls Sigurd and Einar together rally the western part of the army. 'But,' said Einar, 'let us not stand here in the open. Behind us at the steep corner of the Down is the old earthwork fortress. From there we can defy them all.' Sigurd agreed. He saw that King Alfred had halted to rally his soldiers from the wide hill. Sky-Ringer's note rang from beside the King's banner. The men of the shire came to him to form up for the next blow of the battle. They saw the Danes going back, and they marched on pursuing till they came to the earthwork ramparts on the far edge of the Down, over the White Horse cut in the hillside below. Here the heathen made their stand.

A strong wind blew on the hill. King Alfred stood under his flapping flags, and looked at his army about him. He had with him Alfgar and the Dorset men, and all the warriors of his thane-guard. Within the earthwork were a thousand heathen, well-defended.

'Now, Alfgar,' said the King, 'what do you say, and Guntram my friend? Shall we strike now, or wait for Ethelnoth and the rest?'

'I say we can do it now, ourselves,' Alfgar answered. 'We here are strong enough. Give the heathen no time to recover. Go in at once.'

'I think the same,' said Guntram. 'It may be a hard fight but it will be the last. Go in now while we are hot with success, before the wind cools us.'

'So think I,' said the King. 'Sound, Hothric!'

Then once more Hothric sounded the tusk-horn, and once more the Saxon battle-line led by King Alfred went forward to the fierce fight. Once more the shield-wall, the spear-hedge, the bow-storm. The flash of the filed sword-edge striking steel shook the high hill with warfare. The Saxons ran down into the ditch and climbed the bank beyond. Here the heathen with iron welcome waited, their shields heavy with arrows. Horribly hacked were the Saxon helmets. The ringed hauberks broke, the rampart ran with blood. The wolf in the far forest smelt the blood-feast, and his belly hungered. Savagely Sigurd struck down at the climbing men, savagely Einar shared out his own courage with the heathen host around him, standing on the red grass of the rampart. Then said Guntram the Frank:

'Let some of us creep up the bank close to the ground,

hidden under our shield-wall, and let them strike suddenly at the legs and feet of the heathen.'

This was done. Thane Cnebba and some others went up creeping between the Saxons' legs while the battle clashed over them, and struck suddenly at the legs of the foemen on the rampart, and so a gap was made in the heathen line. First through the gap, the King and Guntram gained the rampart's top, and cut a sharp way into the fort. Bracwealla came next, and Escwin and all the King's thanes fighting through the gap to the King's side. Farther along Alfgar also gained the top of the bank, the grim bishop fighting beside him. The banners of Wessex stood now on the rampart top. Fierce now was the fighting. Cnebba fell bleeding, his last fight finished. Jarl Einar killed him. Then came stark Guntram face to face with Einar and they swung out a great circle round them and the sparks flew from their swords. Einar drove Guntram back striking his helmet so that its own dented metal drew blood from Guntram's forehead. Guntram dragged the helmet from his head and flung it full in Einar's face. The jarl bent to avoid it, and Guntram then brought down his sword breaking Einar in shield and shoulder. Einar's own men closed in to guard him, but others of the Saxons came in upon them, and jarl Einar and his men fell fighting all together.

But Guntram now with bare and bloody head cast away his shield and put both hands to his great sword and swinging it led the way forward. On the far bank at the high hill's very edge, against the sky, stark Sigurd stood. Guntram ran at him. They met in deadly fight. The King beat a grim path towards his friend, he and his thanes driving the heathen before them in headlong flight over the far bank and down the steep hill. The Dragon of Wessex came on, and so the last fortress was filled with the Saxons. But still on the farthest edge of the rampart, right above the place where the White Horse is cut in the chalk Sigurd and Guntram fought together. The last of the Danes gathered about them, striking at Guntram all round.

The King and Bracwealla beat their way towards them, all the King's thanes following. They saw the great blow which Sigurd struck, they saw the sword fall from Guntram's hand. Guntram then ran at Sigurd with bare hands, and Sigurd stepped away over the edge and fell rolling over and over down the lofty hill to the bottom. Guntram followed, toppling down, but not far. The last of the heathen had fled, and the King came to the rampart's edge. He saw Guntram below him lying spread out in the middle of the White Horse. He lay head downwards. His blood stained the chalk in a wide river.

King Alfred dropped his sword and scrambled quickly down the steep slope onto the chalk. Bracwealla followed, and together they pulled Guntram over and round till he lay upright. But he lay dead, his face and armour all red and white with blood and chalk.

Bishop Athelheah climbed down to them. Kneeling there in the midst of the White Horse he committed Guntram's soul to God's keeping. Above them on the rampart's edge the thanes of Wessex crowded together and looked down, while the banners of Wessex, the Dragon and the Cross, crowning the top of Ethandune, rustled and tugged on their poles in the strong wind.

CHAPTER THIRTY-EIGHT

Conditions and Advantages

GUTHORM did his best to keep his fugitive troops in order. He rallied as many companies as he could and led them back through the woods to Chippenham. It could hardly be called a march. In scattered lots a third of the Danish army, not more, got themselves back somehow. The rest, those that were left alive, fled away anywhere, mostly back beyond the Mercian border. Wulfric and Ethelnoth pursued the main body, close on their heels. All the heathen stragglers were killed. At Chippenham Guthorm barred the gates and prepared for a defence.

In the evening Jarl Sigurd came back, helmetless and with broken armour, limping with a spear. He was black with blood and bruises.

'You were soon back,' he said to Guthorm scornfully, 'Where do you hide your wounds?' 'What, from falling down a hill?' Guthorm answered. Sigurd did not think Guthorm would have heard of this. Being in pain he could not then find sufficient reply. He went out and nursed his anger.

Before nightfall the first war-bands of the Wessex army were in the fields outside Chippenham. Before morning their whole force was there. The Danes looked out upon a closed circle. They saw King Alfred riding round from company to company, they heard the cheering. Later they saw ditches being dug, shelters being made, tents put up, and they knew the Saxons intended to stay and starve them out. Guthorm reckoned up his store of food, and found only enough for three days at a scrape. The Saxons outside lit their cooking fires, and the villagers from miles around came bringing them food.

King Alfred's tent was pitched under some oak trees. His lords gathered there in council They sat outside in the sun. Bishop Athelheah spoke first. He said:

'King Alfred, a year ago we held council like this at Exeter. We might there have killed Guthorm and all who were with him; but on your decision we spared them. Do you still think that was wise? What will you decide now?'

The King said: 'Lord bishop, God knows I have reason to regret many good friends who have died since Exeter, at least partly because of my decision there. If I was mistaken I do not wish to make the same mistake again. Yet it is a hard question. Tell me now, my lords, what do you think is the chief purpose of these wars we have been fighting?'

They answered: 'To drive the invaders out of Wessex. To keep them out. To keep Christendom and God's Church secure against them.'

'And how can all this be done?' asked the King. 'Will killing alone do it?'

They answered: 'It will help. Have we not now proved it'?

'But,' the King persisted, 'will it help enough? We have now won a great victory, as you say. The hill of Ethandune is covered with dead men. Are they not enough? If not, how many more must we kill? These heathen here are only a handful. Think of all the multitudes of others. There will be no end to it, if killing is the only way.'

Ethelnoth said: 'It was the heathen, not we, who chose the way. If they are for killing, what else can we do?'

The King answered: 'The purpose of battles is not to make more battles, but to make peace. And peace is made with treaties.'

'The heathen never keep their treaties, Lord King,' said Wulfric. 'You know that.'

The King answered: 'If I know anything, I know that the heathen will both take and keep anything they think is to their advantage.' The lords laughed grimly and said: 'That is true enough.'

'So,' said the King, 'if their advantage should be the same as ours, we might all benefit by it. Listen my lords: Great as has been our victory here, you know that we still cannot prevent the heathen from seizing and settling in other parts of the country beyond our borders. It has gone too far, there are too many of them. Some things we must accept as they are, whether we like them or not. But these settlements of the heathen will be a continual threat to us, unless their leaders can be convinced it is to their advantage to keep on good terms with us. What we need, therefore, is for our neighbours to be ruled by someone who, to feel secure, has at least as much need of us as we of him. Then not only would he himself not attack us, but he would stand as a shield between us and the others.'

The lords looked doubtful. 'Among the heathen, how could such a person be found?' said they. 'And, even more, how could he be trusted?'

'It might be possible,' said the King. 'What do you think of Guthorm?'

'Guthorm!' they all exclaimed at once. Wulfric spat. Alfgar laughed. But when the hubbub had died down the King continued:

'The idea is not so foolish as you think. Listen again, my lords: King Guthorm is now in a weak position among his followers, and he knows it. As things stand, they are not likely to follow him much longer. These pirate kingships have shallow loyalties, and seldom outlast the immediate benefits they can give. After such a defeat Guthorm may be lucky not to have his throat cut. But if we act quickly we can help him. If he makes a good treaty with us now, which would be on our own terms, he will have an alliance which will support him in power among his followers for so long as he keeps the peace with us. We should all gain by it.'

Bishop Athelheah rose to his feet. 'Lord King!' he exclaimed. 'An alliance! And with the heathen! Never, Lord King!'

'With the heathen, never, indeed, Lord bishop', answered the King, mildly. 'First it will be necessary for the heathen to be baptised. Guthorm must become a Christian. My Lord, if he could be persuaded to accept Christian baptism from you, could you be persuaded to accept a treaty of alliance with him?'

In the deep silence that followed, suddenly Ethelnoth began to laugh. The bishop frowned.

'Why do you laugh, lord Ethelnoth?' he asked; and the ealdorman answered: 'I was thinking of Guthorm in his christening robe.'

It was indeed as King Alfred had said. In Chippenham Guthorm had begun to make a rueful reckoning of his chieftains, and guessed there were few who would stay with him in his failing fortunes after this, if any got out of it alive. Sigurd did not disguise his hostility, though he was not inclined to rivalry. He was still in pain. He had hurt his back in his fall. Olaf the Skald also lay wounded. He lay in Guthorm's house. He had lost much blood, though now he was recovering. Skafti looked after him. Guthorm said to Olaf: 'When I was a boy I was proud to seek battle and danger in the wars of grown men, but things were going well for us in those days. It is different with Skafti. If I can, I will get him out of this. He has all his life in front of him. King Alfred talks much about a merciful God. Perhaps he might have mercy on boys, if not on men. Perhaps if Skafti became a Christian . . .?' He paused and scratched his beard. 'Well,' he went on, 'King Alfred's Christian luck held out to the end. It did not desert him in his time of misfortune. I wonder, what will he do now? After Exeter, will he ever offer to make terms again? Well, if so, let him send to me. I will not send to him.' This he added defiantly, and with pride; but also, Olaf thought, not without some regret.

King Alfred did not send for several days longer. In fact,

he lay sick in his tent, suffering his old enemy. The weather turned cold. The heathen in Chippenham began to famish. They were in no state for any more fighting, not even for Valhalla. They were glad to receive King Alfred's messengers when at last they came.

Guthorm combed his hair and beard and put on his cap to hide his baldness. He put on his hauberk and his sword and his arm-rings, and all the gear that becomes a king and a warrior. Sigurd and three other chiefs went with him to Alfred's tent. They were courteously received.

CHAPTER THIRTY-EIGHT

Leave-Taking

GUTHORM's baptism took place at midsummer. The ceremony was held at Aller church, in the King's Marsh, within sight of Athelney. Guthorm came there with thirty of his chief men. Sigurd was among them, and Olaf, and Skafti. They had been taken as hostages after the surrender at Chippenham; and this time, as never before, the West Saxons had given no hostages in return.

The heathen hostages had spent their time taking Christian instruction from Bishop Athelheah and his priests. They had to learn the baptismal creed and repeat it by heart, and this some of them did not find easy, though most could manage it in the end without prompting.

A great gathering came to the ceremony. With King Alfred came not only the ealdormen and thanes who had fought at Ethandune, but also the lords of the eastern shires, Berkshire and Sussex and Surrey, now at last recovering from the effect of the heathen invasion. Many churchmen were there. Old Bishop Tunbeort of Winchester came, and young Bishop Wighelm of Selsey. For all this gathering a great camp was made on Aller Hill on the mainland overlooking the causeway which leads across the Marsh to Aller island and the little church.

Midway along the causeway there is a bridge over a shallow stream which drains through the Marsh to the river. At the side of the stream the baptismal laver was dug, a pool waist deep, the bottom covered with a clean layer of stones and sand. Two tents were set up one on each side of the stream leading to and from the laver. These were for the anointings.

For three days before the ceremony Guthorm and the others kept their fast. Then on the third day they came down to the laver, passing in procession through all the company on Aller Hill. They came to the causeway and they stood there, first facing the west. Here they shouted together: 'I renounce thee, Satan, and all thy works and all thy being.' Then they turned to the east and repeated the baptismal creed. Then one by one they entered the first tent, Guthorm leading. They took off all their clothes, and Bishop Wighelm anointed each of them from head to foot with the holy oil. Then they entered the stream and the laver. Three times each of them confessed his new faith and three times Bishop Athelheah with his hand on their head put each of them down into the water. They then came out of the water on the other side, and here old Bishop Tunbeort received them in the second tent, and anointed them again on the forehead, on the ears, on the nose and on the breast with the holy chrism oil. Then he gave each of them the white robe of purity, which each put on. Each had the white baptismal fillet bound round his brow, and over the top of his head in the form of a cross, as all Christians have at their baptism. This must stay upon their heads for seven days. Thus came Guthorm out of the anointing-place, and went up again onto the causeway where his godfather King Alfred awaited him and went with him and all the others to the church on the island. A great Mass was held there to the glory of God, rich with incense and the singing of psalms. The monks and priests, and noblemen of Wessex knelt outside all round the church, which, being so small, could hold only a few. In that church Guthorm received the Sacrament for the first time.

King Alfred had a royal vill at Wedmore, on the northern border of the Marsh, on a hill looking south towards Polden. Here everything was made ready for the feast of the Chrism-Loosing, on the seventh day. Here then came Guthorm and the others, still wearing their baptismal fillets about their brows. King Alfred received them there. He himself unbound the fillet from Guthorm's head, and gave him the baptismal name, by which he has since been known. He named him Athelstan.

Thus was King Athelstan Red-Beard, my godfather, born into the Christian world. At the great feast with which they were welcomed, the Christian Danes became very drunk and merry, but no harm came of that. Only Jarl Sigurd was morose, because his back still pained him, in spite of his christening, which he had hoped would do it some good. King Alfred sent his leech to him, who bathed his back with certain herb-oils which soothed it. He was never entirely cured of the trouble, however.

Athelstan and his Danes stayed twelve days at Wedmore. He received many gifts from King Alfred, and together with their counsellors they sat for long hours making the treaty to which in the end they both set their hands. Because of this treaty the borders of Wessex were never again violated by the Danes, and because of it King Athelstan ruled securely in East Anglia until the day he died, many years after, suddenly, sitting upright upon his horse.

The Lady Elswitha came from Sherborne to the feast at Wedmore. Hildis and Elred came with her. So at Wedmore they were reunited once more with their brother Elric, a man now, who had been in his first battle. As the three walked together on the hill overlooking the Marsh in the warm air of the June evening, watching the swallows flying back and forth around the high roof of the King's hall, they came round a corner and met face to face with Skafti, and Olaf his father. They would have passed by, but Skafti and Elric looked into each other's faces, and suddenly recognized each other. They had come thus face to face once before; but then they were shadowed under their battle-helmets on Ethandune field. Now they stopped, and each took the other by the hand. Hildis was standing near. She looked at young Skafti and he at her; and she then looked down. Elric said: 'This is my sister.' Olaf put his hand on Skafti's shoulder and they moved away, but as they went round the corner of the building Skafti looked back, and saw the girl Hildis looking back also over her shoulder. This was the first meeting of Hildis and Skafti, here by the Great Marsh, with the swallows flying over it back and forth between Wedmore and Athelney in the summer evening. Some years later they met again and did not part. They were wed. These, as I have told you, were my parents.

My grandmother Waltruda remained with the nuns at Donhead, and went with them when King Alfred built the new convent for them at Shaftesbury, nearby. She served very humbly there. She would not accept any high position. The King later gave back to her the property of Alham, but she in turn gave it and all its revenues to the convent. I once saw her myself when I was a young man of twenty. She was a white-haired old lady, very stern and saintly. She still spoke with a slight trace of her Frankish accent. She stayed a summer with us in East Anglia. She had had permission to leave the convent to see her children again before she grew too old to travel such great distances. After her return she remained in the convent for the rest of her life. She lived to be eighty-three, so it is said.

She never again saw her foster-son Edgar. He, after the defeat of his one-time protectors at Ethandune, fled from England with his wife Edith and their new-born baby. They went first to Flanders, to Count Baldwin's palace, where Edgar saw his mother Judith once again, for the last time. She, as I have said, had grown very fat and had many children. She gave Edgar money and clothes and horses, and sent him with a letter to her brother Lewis, who had become Emperor of the Franks. But it was not a good time to go there, for in that same year Lewis died, and the Frankish Empire was riven apart with civil wars. The story of all the kings and counter-kings and all the divisions and dissensions that followed is beyond telling. Edgar travelled hither and thither with Edith his wife, of whom he had grown fond, and all their numerous children. In the end I have heard he took service with his mother's cousin,

Berengar, Duke of Friuli, from whom he held lands in Italy. I know no more of him. He may still be living.

When the twelve days of the feast of Wedmore were over King Athelstan took leave of his godfather King Alfred for the last time, and rode away with Sigurd and the rest, back into Mercia. From there he went to East Anglia where he established his kingdom. King Alfred later sent him a trained scribe, so that they could correspond by letters, and this they did for many years.

At Athelney King Alfred founded a monastery. He himself visited it often. Whenever he returned from there towards Winchester and the Eastern shires he travelled always by the same road. Sometimes he would take Alfred Dane-Leg, his secretary, with him. They would ride the ancient trackway through Selwood to King's Seat Hill, ascending there to the Plain. At King Egbert's Stone they would turn north and ride once more the way to Iley Wood and Ethandune.

Long gone from there is any sign of armies and dead men. The last rusted weapon was found and carried off years ago. The Ethandune grass is cropped short by flocks of sheep.

At the far north-west corner of the Down, where the ancient earthwork crowns the edge of the hill above the steep side of the White Horse, King Alfred, with the secretary, his Namesake, would dismount and go and stand on the windy summit looking out over the whole wide region below, the country where once Guthorm and his vikings had roamed, holding for a while all Wessex and all Christendom in peril. Here, at this corner of the hill, under the rampart, Guntram the Frank lies sleeping.

About the Author

C. WALTER HODGES has spent most of his professional life as a graphic artist. In the field of book illustration alone he has more than seventy titles to his credit. He won the 1964 Kate Greenaway Award for his *Shakespeare's Theatre* illustrations But his interests are wide, and he has applied himself with equal enthusiasm to the designing of exhibitions, to mural decoration and especially to designing scenery and costumes for films and productions. He was one of the original designers of the Mermaid Theatre in London. He is a recognized authority on the structure of Shakespeare's Globe Theatre and has published books and articles on the subject. His first children's book – *Columbus Sails* – was written during a visit to New York. The B.B.C. reviewer said at the time that 'it deserves to live for many years and become, in fact, a minor classic'. And so it has, both here and in the United States.

The Marsh King completes the story of King Alfred which was begun in *The Namesake* (also in Puffins), and so ends a study which has occupied Walter Hodges for a number of years, and he says that although these books are to be read as fiction, not history, he is satisfied that the story does not depart in any important way from the facts of history, so far as these are known.

Some other Puffins you might enjoy

MASTER ENTRICK

Michael Mott

One cold blustery night in 1754 young Robert Entrick, as he rode home across the Lancashire Moors, suddenly felt afraid, though it was easy on such a night to hear things behind the wind. Then two figures on horseback came up out of the darkness towards him. Someone made a grab at his reins, someone struck him, and he slipped sideways...

A few months later, having been brutally transported to America where his new master was murdered by Indians, Robert escaped. He was free, on his own, with a few wet rags to wear, a short hoe, and a stolen canoe. Here in the middle of America, with its woods full of murderous savages, he was more shipwrecked than Robinson Crusoe. And Robert Entrick, who had once been afraid of riding alone in the dark, felt only a wave of elation.

I AM DAVID

Anne Holm

David lay quite still in the darkness of the concentration camp, waiting for the signal. 'You must get away tonight,' the man had told him. 'Stay awake so that you're ready just before the guard is changed. When you see me strike a match, the current will be cut off and you can climb over – you'll have half a minute, no more. Follow the compass southwards till you get to Salonica and then find a ship that's bound for Italy, and then go north till you come to a country called Denmark – you'll be safe there.'

So David, who had known no other life but that of the concentration camp, escaped into a world he knew nothing of, not even what things to eat nor how to tell good men from bad.

A deeply moving story, highly recommended for readers of 11 and over.

THE HOUSE OF SIXTY FATHERS

Meindert DeJong

Little Tien Pao had never seen guns or motor cars or aeroplanes until the Japanese destroyed his village. He escaped up the river with his father, mother, baby sister, and pet pig 'Glory of the Republic', but while they were away looking for food the sampan broke its moorings and took him back to Japanese occupied territory.

The rest of the story is about his almost unbelievable courage and endurance as he searches for them. He is in a Japanese bombing attack, saves a shot down American airman and is hunted for two days and nights. He is helped by Chinese guerrillas, who take him back to the town where he left his parents, only to discover it has become an army of terrified refugees. He keeps vigil on the roadside until, dying from hunger, he is found by more airmen. They take him to camp and offer to adopt him, but Tien Pao knows he must go on looking . . .

EARTHFASTS

William Mayne

At the dusk of a summer's day, Keith Heseltine and David Wix were still out on Haw Bank, investigating something. There was a new mound in the grass, and it was getting bigger. Then the ground stirred, as if someone were getting out of bed. And with the movement came the sound of drumming. David was trembling all over, and so was Keith, and then they made sense of it. All that had come out of the hill was a boy about their own size, with a drum.

Two hundred years before, Nellie Jack John the drummer boy had gone to explore the passage under the castle, looking for King Arthur with his sleeping knights. Now he had come out again, but time had got mixed up, so that the ancient dead giants were walking about again, and domestic pigs were transformed into dangerous wild swine.

PIG IN THE MIDDLE

William Mayne

Michael followed the other boys. John took out his keys and opened the door in the wall. Inside the door was darkness. Then Michael began to see, and to hear. He heard water moving. He saw light on the water, and light under the water. In the water was an empty barge, tar black in the dim light.

'This is Pig,' said John. 'It's written on one end of it. Do you swear to help us to sail it to Holland? Emigrate?'

'I do,' said Michael.

And he had sworn away not only his brother, but the rest of his family and everything he knew.

MY SIDE OF THE MOUNTAIN

Jean George

'I am on my mountain in a tree home that people have passed without ever knowing I am here. The house is a hemlock tree six feet in diameter. I came upon it last summer and dug and burnt it out until I made a snug home in the tree.

'My bed is on the right. On the left is a small fireplace with a chimney that leads the smoke out through a knothole. It snowed all day yesterday and today. It must be below zero outside, and yet I can sit here inside my tree and write with bare hands. It is the fourth of December, I think. It is eight months since I ran away from home.'

This is part of Sam Gribley's diary. Sam had escaped from his family's cramped flat in New York and his eight brothers and sisters to live on the barren farm his grandfather had owned in the Catskill Mountains. He had a pen-knife, an axe, a ball of string, and some flint and steel, and that was all.

APPLICATION FOR MEMBERSHIP OF THE PUFFIN CLUB

TO: THE PUFFIN CLUB SECRETARY,
PENGUIN BOOKS LTD,
HARMONDSWORTH, MIDDLESEX

Please enrol me in the Puffin Club. I enclose my subscription for (please tick appropriate box)

Three Year Membership (£1)* ☐

One Year Membership (10s.)* ☐

Family Membership, 10s. a year plus 2s. 6d. for each extra member.* ☐

Overseas Membership
School Membership } Please apply for further details.

(Write clearly in block letters)

Christian name(s) Surname

Full Address (use a separate box for each line)

Boy or Girl.................................Date of Birth..............................

Signature...

* Subject to alteration without prior notice.